# Social Media Ethics
# Made Easy

# Social Media Ethics Made Easy

## How to Comply with FTC Guidelines

Joseph W. Barnes

 BUSINESS EXPERT PRESS

First published in 2016 by
Business Expert Press, LLC
222 East 46th Street, New York, NY 10017
www.businessexpertpress.com

ISBN-13: 978-1-60649-852-1 (paperback)
ISBN-13: 978-1-60649-853-8 (e-book)

Business Expert Press Giving Voice to Values on Business Ethics and Corporate Social Responsibility Collection

Collection ISSN: 2333-8806 (print)
Collection ISSN: 2333-8814 (electronic)

Cover and interior design by S4Carlisle Publishing Services Private Ltd., Chennai, India

First edition: 2016

10 9 8 7 6 5 4 3 2 1

Printed in the United States of America.

# Dedication

*Dedicated to My Students, Peers, and*
*My Children*
*Chris, Kim, and Jenny*

—Joseph W. Barnes

# Abstract

When you go to buy a product online, book travel, or research a service, do you read the customer reviews? Do you count on those reviews to be from real customers? If you said, yes, then you are like most of us. The problem is that today's reviews have been infiltrated with fake reviews and fake testimonials. It's hard to tell a real review from a fake review in a world where we count on trust and rely more on each other than traditional marketing messages.

This book is about truth—how to understand a real review from a fake review, why it is important to establish a social media policy at every business and organization, and how to create that policy.

Until the Federal Trade Commission started cracking down, there were even cases of people marketing themselves as "reviewers" on YouTube. They would happily submit reviews for just $5 or $10 each.

But it gets much more serious. In New York, the Attorney General cracked down on restaurants that were hiring people to submit fake reviews.

Over the last several years, as the use of social media has increased, we have seen many instances of ethics violations from fake online reviews, to testimonial posts by people connected with a brand but not revealing the connection, to tweets that try to turn a tragedy into a marketing event. This has prompted a call for ethics training in social media. That is one of the key reasons for this book.

At the same time, the Federal Trade Commission has created a series of "strict" guidelines that instruct businesses and organizations to disclose specific information to protect consumers in ways that are *"clear and conspicuous."*

In this book *Social Media Ethics Made Easy*, we explain the current social/digital marketing landscape, describe why we need social media ethics standards, and how to create and implement a social media ethics policy for your business or organization.

# Keywords

Federal Trade Commission disclosure, FTC disclosure, Federal Trade Commission Endorsement, FTC Endorsement, FTC endorsement requirements, Federal Trade Commission social media, FTC social media, Federal Trade Commission social media rules, FTC social media rules, Social media deception, social media disclosure, Social media endorsements, social media marketing

# Contents

# Introduction

First, let me get your attention:

"One in four people globally use social networks and by 2020, there will be more than six devices per person in the world." (Knezevich 2014)

If you work for a business (for-profit, nonprofit, education, or faith based), you now work for a media publishing business because every business now uses social media. That is why this book is important to you, your reputation, your career, and your business.

This book is about *your* future and your reputation. It is about one simple word: *trust*.

It is about your rights as a consumer to know when a post on a social media platform is an "advertisement" or a true testimonial. It is also about knowing whether a post that sounds so favorable is by a consumer who loves the product or service, or is by an "insider" simply disguised as a customer. It is about your ability to easily know the difference at a glance.

Why is this so important? It is important because social media posts by "insiders" can easily mislead you and other consumers. Here is an example:

You see a movie review on a website. The person recommends the film and has incredible things to say. It sounds legit, but what if you went to see the film and it did not live up to the review? Perhaps because the "reviewer" was actually the theater manager who books the films for that theater. Would you feel let down? Would that post have been more honest and transparent if the "reviewer" had disclosed the fact that he or she was the person who books the films?

Here is another example. Have you read some of the book reviews or product reviews on Amazon.com? What if someone reviewed a book or a product you were interested in but never disclosed they were part of the public relations team hired by the company that distributes the book or manufactures the product? Would you feel that was unethical? Now I'm sure this never happens but what if it did? How would you feel if you bought the book or product, it didn't live up to its review, and later you found out the "reviewer" was hired to write reviews on as many sites as possible?

This book is about open, honest disclosure. It is a guidebook to help you understand the importance of and how to disclose your product, service, or venue on social media platforms, in an ethical way.

This is not about theory. It is about a reality that faces all of us every day.

We live in a new era. Not only must we disclose our relationship to employers and the public when we post on social media, in our businesses and organizations, we must also listen and respond to consumers.

We live in a time when consumers have more power than businesses and organizations. One consumer can post a negative tweet, picture, or video online, and if it goes viral, it does substantial damage to a business.

Perhaps the most classic case that demonstrates this point is the infamous *"United Breaks Guitars"* case.

If you know the case, it is a great reminder, and if you are unfamiliar with the story, it is now a case study from Harvard to universities and professionals worldwide. It is an example demonstrating how one person with a $150 video can get the attention of consumers and a multibillion-dollar corporation.

Let us go back in time to 2009. Canadian musician Dave Carroll was traveling on United Airlines and claimed the airline had broken one of his Taylor guitars. He also claimed that he and other passengers had seen baggage handlers throwing guitar cases on the tarmac during a layover at O'Hare Airport in Chicago. When he arrived at his destination, he discovered his $3,500 Taylor guitar was severely damaged.

As Carroll tells the story in interviews and in a video he later posted on YouTube, he spent nine months trying to work out compensation with United Airlines with no avail. He said United Airlines informed him he did not qualify for compensation because he did not file a claim within the "standard 24-hour timeframe."

Therefore, Carroll (2012) and his band members, the Sons of Maxwell, created and posted a music video about his experience called *"United Breaks Guitars."* The video immediately drew attention of bloggers, the news media, and many on social media platforms; within days, it went viral and became mainstream news.

"Within four days of the video being posted online, United Airlines' stock price fell ten percent, costing stockholders about $180 million in value." (Ayres 2009)

As of 2014, the United Breaks Guitars video had been seen over 14 million times on YouTube and is now a book!

In this book, we will review the Federal Trade rules and guidelines, explain why they affect all of us, help guide you in setting up a social media policy for any organization, and help you as a consumer.

We will also share what is happening in the rapidly changing world of privacy and help you understand what is happening now and in the future.

Whether you are someone who has a Facebook account, a student learning about why ethics and social media are so important, a businessperson who wants to implement a social media policy, or a social media guru, this book is for you.

Let us put it this way, if *you* value your privacy and want to be respected in this world, then read on.

Think how many times Facebook has changed its privacy settings without telling you. Have these changes ever caught you off guard? Is that ethical?

Have you ever vented in the heat of the moment and wished you had not said something? Imagine how teachers, physicians, lawyers, and students feel when they do that on social media.

There Is No Such Thing as Delete!

Contrary to what you may think, **there is *no* delete button**. No matter what you think, whether you like it or not, nothing you post online, send via e-mail, or text is ever fully deleted. From employers, to Google, and many more, there is a digital record of everything you post and every picture that gets uploaded.

There is a side benefit in the discussions about social media ethics: These talks include an opportunity for every business to reinforce the values they stand for.

In this book, we will review what is happening in the social/digital space, and why this is so important to you. This background is important before understanding the ethical issues.

As I said in the beginning of this introduction, this book is about one word: *trust.*

Disclaimer: I am not a lawyer; I am an academic, consultant, and a consumer. Before making any changes to your existing policies, please consult with your own legal counsel and human resources experts.

# CHAPTER 1

# The Social, Digital, and Mobile Landscape

## Let's Look at the Social/Digital Landscape

Why is this topic important? Because billions of people use social/digital media each day. This is how we communicate, share, review, and vent. It is now the digital fabric of our lives.

To fully understand and appreciate social/digital media, we need to understand how prevalent it has become and who is using the platforms.

Worldwide, there are over two billion people who use social media.

According to the PEW Internet Research Project, 76 percent of online adults use social networking sites (PewResearchCenter 2015).

The PEW data also shows, "The growing ubiquity of cell phones, especially the rise of smartphones, has made social networking just a finger tap away. Fully 40 percent of cell phone owners use a social networking site on their phone, and 28 percent do so on a typical day." (PewResearch-Center 2014)

Have you found yourself connected to your smartphone from morning until night? You are not alone.

According to the U.S. Commerce department, "Eighty-eight percent of Americans ages 25 and older used mobile phones. Mobile Internet usage has grown substantially across demographic categories." (U.S. Department of Commerce and NTIA 2014)

Users include readers and viewers, curators of content, news sources, politicians, almost every major company in America, nonprofits, and educational institutions. Ages range from the very young to a 114-year-old woman who has to lie about age to join Facebook. (Shah 2014)

As we look at the different platforms, Facebook is still the most dominant in the social media space, despite all the other platforms that have surfaced. According to BusinessInsider.com (Guimarães 2014),

- Facebook skews significantly female. Women in the United States are more likely to use Facebook than men by about 10 percentage points, according to a 2013 survey of social network adoption.
- Facebook remains the top social network for U.S. teens. Nearly half of teen Facebook users say they are using the site more, and Facebook has more daily teen users than any other social network.
- Instagram has edged out Facebook and Twitter in terms of *prestige* among young users. U.S. teens now describe Instagram as "most important," while Facebook and Twitter lost ground on this measure, according to Piper Jaffray's twice yearly teen survey. The survey also found that 83 percent of U.S. teens in wealthy households were on Instagram.
- LinkedIn is actually more popular than Twitter among U.S. adults. LinkedIn's core demographic are those aged between 30 and 49, that is those in the prime of their career-rising years. Not surprisingly, LinkedIn also has a pronounced skew toward well-educated users.
- Twitter has begun to lean toward male users, whereas previously it was a more gender-balanced social network. Pew found that 22 percent of men use Twitter, while only 15 percent of women tweet.
- YouTube reaches more adults aged 18 to 34 than any single cable TV network. Nearly half of people in this age group visited YouTube between December 2013 and February 2014, according to Nielsen. It was rated by Millennials as the top place to watch content, ahead of digital and TV properties like Facebook and ESPN.
- Snapchat is the youngest social network of all. More than 6 out of 10 Snapchat users are in the 18-to-24 age group,

compared to 28 percent of Instagram users, according to a survey by Informate.

(Information above from Guimarães 2014)

The use of social media goes far beyond the facts and figures. Social media is the fabric of society because it allows us to share and create community. Whether we are sharing events and moments of pride on Facebook, fast-moving developments on Twitter, "how to" videos on YouTube, online reviews, or simply fun (or sometimes embarrassing) moments on other platforms, social media has become intertwined with our lives. Today, we now carry the Internet in our pockets or purses 24/7. Social media is how we listen and share, in our personal lives and in business.

We can examine this trend from a variety of vantage points including sociology, psychology, technology, and interpersonal communications. We can seek to analyze the trends to death, but that is not what this book is about. It is about how we use, and misuse, the digital landscape, how to understand the ethical standards that should be in place when using social media, and how to create a social media policy.

Technology has opened the door for sharing like never before. Instead of sharing an experience you have had with your friends, you can now share it with hundreds of friends and followers who can share it with their friends and followers. If it's big enough, it will spread like a wildfire and become viral, which can be good or bad, depending upon the content and the impact.

It's important to understand the speed at which information flows today. We now live in a 24/7 *real-time* world. We can buy almost anything we want at any hour of the day or night online. Likewise, we can share whatever we want 24/7.

For businesses used to operating in traditional ways, today's digital landscape can be frightening. For businesses that get it, the digital landscape presents untapped opportunities.

Consumer anger can travel at digital light speed. This quantum development means that angry consumers now vent in real time instead of writing letters or calling businesses to complain. Instead of only telling a few people about a negative experience, even the shyest person on earth with a computer and hundreds of followers can do damage to a business.

This is only the beginning. Social and digital media are still in their infancy. It wasn't until the mid-1990s that the first online shopping sites widely appeared.

Just for grins, there's a now famous *Newsweek* article from the mid-1990s headlined as follows:

*The Internet? Bah! Hype alert: Why cyberspace isn't, and will never be, nirvana"*

Today, hardly a night goes by without the major news networks citing content from social media sources.

At the same time, a report released from the U.S. Commerce Department's National Telecommunications and Information Administration (NTIA) found, "Americans are rapidly embracing mobile Internet devices such as smart phones and tablet computers for a wide range of activities beyond just voice communications, such as checking email and using social networks." (U.S. Department of Commerce and NTIA 2014)

## Apps Rule

How many apps are on your smartphone? I have over 20 that provide calendar, news, weather, and shopping shortcuts.

"Apps today are driving the majority of media consumption activity, now accounting for 7 out of every 8 minutes of media consumption on mobile devices. On smartphones, app activity is even higher, at 88-percent usage versus 82-percent on tablets. More than half (57-percent) use apps every single day, while 26-percent of tablet owners do. And 79 percent of smartphone owners use apps nearly every day, saying they use them at least 26 days per month, versus 52-percent for tablet users." (Perez 2014)

## Digital Consumers

These digital devices and easy access have changed our lives and our behavior.

According to the A.C. Nielsen Company, "Americans now own four digital devices on average, and the average U.S. consumer spends 60 hours a week consuming content across devices. And a majority of U.S. households now own high-definition televisions (HDTVs), Internet-connected computers and smartphones. In addition to more devices, consumers also have more choices for how and when they access content. As a result, consumption habits are changing. The rapid adoption of a second screen has transformed the traditional TV viewing experience, with consumers using smartphones and tablets in ways that are natural extensions of the programming they watch. And social media usage is now standard practice in our daily lives—almost half (47 percent) of smartphone owners visit social networks every day." (nielsen.com 2014a)

## Hispanics are Ahead of the Digital Curve

In the social/digital space, there are some cultural differences. "Hispanic consumers have rapidly adopted multiple-screens into their daily video viewing routines and represent 47 million traditional TV viewers in the U.S. and growing. Latinos adopt smartphones at a higher rate than any other demographic group and watch more hours of videos online and on their mobile phones than the average American." (nielsen.com 2014a)

## Tablets, Airplanes, and Cars!

As you read this, new innovations in tablets are being developed each week, more airlines are outfitting planes for Wi-Fi, and cars are now being sold with Internet access.

It would have been crazy to think of cars with Internet access just a few years ago, but now, the technology is here and that *will* affect social media.

"Cars are big business and when you consider how personal a car purchase is, new connectivity features are helping automakers personalize content for everyone, from working moms in need of hands-free talk to twenty-something singles looking to score reservations at the local hotspot." (nielsen.com 2014b)

"The modern car offers some form of connectivity for everyone—and that appeal is growing. In fact, of the 44-percent of future auto intenders who plan to purchase a new car within the next two years, 39-percent are very likely to purchase a connected car with built-in features. The rise in connectivity options—whether for getting directions or checking engine diagnostics—also presents a unique opportunity for advertisers and marketers to reach consumers in the comfort of their own cockpits." (nielsen. com 2014b)

## Mobile Payments

What are we talking about now? Mobile payments, of course. In 2014, Apple announced Apple Pay, its new mobile payments system.

The worldwide mobile payment revenue in 2015 was 450 billion U.S. dollars and is expected to surpass 1 trillion U.S. dollars in 2019. (Statistica 2016)

MasterCard and PRIME Research released a study, which tracked more than 13 million social media comments across Twitter, Facebook, online blogs, and forums around the world. The study shows improved sentiment toward mobile payments and rapid growth in consumer use and merchant acceptance. While security concerns around mobile payments still exist, the study demonstrates that consumers and merchants have moved from "why use mobile payments?" to "which mobile payment option should be used?" (newsroom.mastercard.com 2014)

What does this mean? According to Ritesh Gupta in transactionworld. net, "One can look forward to a seamless environment where consumers can also perform transactions in addition to their daily social conversation." (transactionworld.net 2014)

Eran Savir, CEO/cofounder, SeatID, a social seating and booking platform that adds social widgets and data to ticketing and booking websites and apps says, "Socializing is a key element in the decision-making process in every aspect of our lives. A rapidly increasing number of people share and socialize online as part of a cognitive process that helps them make up their minds in regard to what products to buy, which hotels to book, how to travel, etc." (transactionworld.net 2014)

"Business owners understand that their users are social animals, that these people ask their friends for recommendations on Facebook, that they want to know where their peers are going," Savir added. "Business proprietors understand that it is to their definite advantage to encourage potential customers to bring social experience to their online purchasing processes. Though it's not yet a mature concept, I have no doubt that in five years from now, social proofing is going to be broadly implemented." (transactionworld.net 2014)

## Social TV

This is one of the latest technological advances that facilitates social media on a user's TV set.

The Council for Research Excellence (CRE) released a study about socially connected TV viewing. The study found that 16 percent of prime-time TV viewing involved some sort of real-time engagement with social media. Further, "during nearly half of these occasions (7.3-percent of primetime TV viewing instances), the viewer is engaging with social media specifically about the show being viewed. Socially connected TV viewing was highest for new programs. Facebook and Twitter were the two primary social networks involved in real-time socially connected TV interactions." (Sterling 2014)

The CRE also found that "The most important determining factor among consumers in purchasing a new TV or video device is the ability for it to connect to the Internet and stream content." (researchexcellence. com 2014)

## Summary

In this chapter, we have learned about the dramatic and rapid growth of social and digital media. We now have a better understanding of who is engaged in social media, how and why they are using the platforms and content. Moving forward, we will look at defining ***social media*** in an ever-changing social/digital landscape.

# CHAPTER 2

# Defining Social Media

Defining social media is like trying to define the Internet, in part, because the technology, platforms, and use of the platforms are in constant evolution. Who would have thought just 16 years ago that we would have powerful platforms such as Facebook, Twitter, YouTube, Instagram, Pinterest, LinkedIn, Google+, Vine, Tumblr, Flickr, and more?

We also have technology that has given us real-time sharing opportunities, through mobile apps.

Social media is by its very nature about **sharing, the creation of community, and interaction.** Social media is about being social, it is about **a participatory culture**, whether on a large scale or small scale. There are people who consume social media content, there are people who share, and there are people who create content. This results in an enormous amount of information being shared, some positive, some negative, some personal, some about businesses and organizations. Like it or not, social media is the future of communication.

Brian Solis, a digital analyst, anthropologist, and futurist studies the effects of disruptive technology on business and society. Solis (2012) believes we should think about social media in a broad perspective:

"We should think about social media and mobile behavior as it's related to psychology, anthropology, communication, economics, human geography, ethnography, et al. After all, everything comes down to people. Unfortunately, in new media, we tend to put technology ahead of people." (Solis 2012)

"Relationships are not a function or derivative of technology. At best, the definition of relationships when technology is at the center of connectivity, can mean nothing more than the way in which two or more concepts, objects, or people are connected, or the state of being connected.

Relationships are not static. They are in fact dynamic and becoming more so every day." (Solis 2012)

We share both the good and the bad experiences online just as we do in person with family, friends, and coworkers.

"The connected evaluate shared experiences of those they trust, and expect businesses to respond to their socialized questions. As a consequence, they don't follow a linear approach through the classic 'interest to intent' funnel during their decision making process. Rather, they follow an elliptical pattern where their next steps are inspired by the insights of others, and their experiences are, in turn, fed back into the cycle to inform the decisions of others." (Solis 2012)

Social media is a force that has changed our lives. We keep in touch like never before through social media; we share pictures and videos at unprecedented rates; we post reviews of products we like and dislike for thousands to see; and if we are an unhappy consumer, we can tweet our dislike and even share a picture for thousands to read. As consumers, the power has shifted from a push mentality by marketers to interactivity requiring smart businesses to listen and respond. We also make mistakes, as individuals and as businesses. In part, that is why we need to study social media ethics, understand what is appropriate, what is not appropriate, and why every business and organization needs to have a social media ethics policy in place.

## Enter: The Power of Word-of-Mouth Recommendations and Online Reviews

How powerful are word-of-mouth recommendations and reviews in person and online?

"According to a study from marketing firm Lithium Technologies, one third of Americans said they don't trust advertising to give them information about a product or service they are interested in buying. More than two-thirds of the respondents in the U.S. said they were more receptive to recommendations from family and friends than to online advertising, the study found." (Wall Street Journal 2014)

*"According to Nielsen, 92-percent of consumers believe recommendations from friends and family over all forms of advertising."* (Whitler 2014)

This is an incredibly powerful statistic. Just think about this for a moment. Over 90 percent of us trust recommendations from family and friends over all forms of advertising. In addition, we trust online product and service reviews from people we don't even know, more than traditional advertising. This is why, it's so important to help businesses and organizations understand the importance of establishing social media ethical guidelines.

Consumers are evolving faster than businesses can keep up with them. Why? Because we live in a 24/7-connected world.

As we proceed in this book, let me quote from parts of NPR's code of ethics,

"The Internet and the social media communities it encompasses can be incredible resources. They offer both a remarkably robust amount of historical material and an incredible amount of 'real-time' reporting from people at the scenes of breaking news events. But they also present new and unfamiliar challenges, and they tend to amplify the effects of any ethical misjudgments you might make. So tread carefully. Conduct yourself online just as you would in any other public circumstances. Treat those you encounter online with fairness, honesty and respect, just as you would offline. Be honest about your intent." (ethics.npr.org n.d.)

## Summary

In this chapter, we have learned that the definition of social media is evolving based on new technologies, platforms, and applications. However, the constant is that social media is about sharing. As humans, we have a need to share the good, the bad, and the ugly. We do it in person, and now in greater numbers, we do it online.

We also learned that over 90 percent of consumers now trust recommendations from family and friends—and yes even from online reviewers we've never met—more than traditional advertising.

# CHAPTER 3

# Defining Ethics

Ethics is about doing the right thing, but in today's digital world, doing what's right is not always clear, especially from workplace to workplace, organization to organization, and so on. That is why it is so important to define ethics in this book, and in your organization.

Even the prestigious Ethics Resources Center acknowledges the challenge of defining "ethics."

"Even among those who believe they know ethics, there is not total agreement on the meaning of the terms that are used. For many, a particular definition is a function of the academic discipline that shaped one's thinking and the religious, theological or philosophical underpinnings of one's personal belief system. For others, there may be a usage that is specific to their individual area of work or study." (Ethics.org 2009)

The Ethics Resources Center proposes this definition: "The decisions, choices, and actions (behaviors) we make that reflect and enact our values." (Ethics.org 2009)

In the social/digital/mobile world, it is about creating social media ethics policies, upholding policies that every business and organization should put in place, being honest, and disclosing relationships such as who you work for in personal posts when endorsing products and services, and not writing fake reviews.

As we will explore throughout this book, much of the social media ethical issues surround posts related to work.

The National Business Ethics Survey (NBES) (Ethics.org 2013) surveyed employees nationwide about social media; the findings are quite revealing.

- More than 1 in 10 employees are "Active Social Networkers" (ASNs) who spend at least 30 percent of their workday linked up to one or more networks.
- Nearly 3 out of 4 social networkers (72 percent) say they spend at least some time on their social networks during every workday, and almost 3 in 10 (28 percent) say such activity adds up to an hour or more of each day they spend at work. Very little of the online time is work related.
- Social networkers are clearly breaking old barriers and talking more freely than ever before about their jobs and their company.
- 6 of 10 ASNs would comment on their personal sites about their company if it was in the news, 53 percent say they share information about work projects once a week or more, and more than a third say they often comment, on their personal sites, about managers, coworkers, and even clients. As a result, workplace "secrets" are no longer secrets, and management must assume that anything that happens at work, that is any new policy, product, or problem, could become publicly known at almost any time.

Mary C. Gentile, Ph.D., author of *Giving Voice to Values*, Director of the Giving Voice to Values curriculum, and senior research scholar at Babson College explains it this way:

"The challenge appears to be not just one of recognizing ethical issues when they arise or learning to think them through—we are all practiced from toddler age with the skill of generating rationalizations for our choices. The challenge, rather, appears to be one of preparing for action: what do you do and say once you know what you think is right?" (Gentile 2010)

As you read this book, it's important to think critically about ethics issues that have arisen in social media and to think about issues that may come up in the future. One group that studies ethics is the Markkula Center for Applied Ethics at Santa Clara University. The experts there pose some interesting questions for all of us to think about. These questions cover areas such as the utilitarian perspective, rights perspective, fairness perspective, and a common good perspective.

- "Do social networkers have a right to privacy?"
- "More and more users of Facebook are finding that prospective employers are perusing their sites, despite the fact that they may conceive of their online presence as personal space." Is this practice ethical?
- "What is a private person's right to control the images and information about them available on line?"
- Are there ways to structure online communities so that they better promote the common good of their members?

## Summary

In this chapter, we have learned that ethics is about doing what is right. In social media, this means disclosing whom you work for in personal posts, about the products or services you have a direct connection with. If you are employed by $X$ company, it's important to say that when writing a glowing post so readers understand the context.

Finally, we learned never to post or participate in any fake reviews.

# CHAPTER 4

# Why This Book Is Necessary

## The Evidence

Why is this book necessary you ask? Because we have seen everything from fake reviews online, to overzealous tweets and posts that cross into unethical territory, to people at businesses and organizations not knowing they are even required by the Federal Trade Commission to disclose relationships with employers when posting about their products or services. I am still shocked that nearly every business I visit, whether for-profit, nonprofit, higher education or faith based, does not know that they are required to have a social media policy and train their employees in social media ethics.

Over the last few years, I have been gathering examples that demonstrate how not to use social media; many of these happen to come from the world of marketing. I show these in my university classes to help set the stage for a more thorough understanding why a social media ethics policy is needed.

These examples are not meant to speak negatively about brands or businesses, but rather to reinforce some key points:

1. The need for social media ethics policies by all businesses and organizations
2. The need for social media ethics training by all businesses, for-profit, nonprofit, higher education, and faith based

Why are policies and training needed? So each business and organization can establish rules or guidelines for social media use by employees, volunteers, board members, vendors, and others.

Even with social media policies and Federal Trade Commission guidelines, we have seen businesses and organizations do stupid things.

"With around a fifth of the world's population on Facebook and some 20 million people joining Twitter every month, social media has provided a new battleground for brands vying for our affection, our advocacy and our money. Unfortunately, this mentality has led to some businesses intentionally overstepping the mark in order to garner competitive advantage. The worst offenders will use Search Engine Optimization (SEO) techniques, for example, to hide negative results; will delete negative reviews, posts and comments; create fake accounts and post positive reviews; pay for 'likes' and fans on Facebook; or leverage 'click farms'." (Brown 2014)

In 2009 "It was revealed that consumer products manufacturer Belkin was exposed for paying people to leave positive reviews on their products via Amazon. The recent Brit Awards also saw social media controversy as journalists were invited to attend on the condition that they shared pre-determined tweets about the sponsor MasterCard." (Brown 2014)

## Paying for Followers May Cost You a Job

If you are reading this, looking for a job, and think you will impress a hiring manager by having an impressive number of followers on LinkedIn and Twitter, think again how you go about it.

Chereen Zaki tells an interesting story with lessons to be learned. As the story goes, her husband was discussing a potential job with her that required him to have a high number of Twitter followers.

In her research she discovered that anyone could "buy" up to 1,000 new Twitter followers in packages for as little as $20. The problem is that it is unethical and you can get caught.

"Employers can now weed out the imposters on Twitter using applications such as Statuspeople.com's Fakers application, or Social Baker's Fake Followers application. These applications allow you to measure your own, as well as other's fake, inactive, and good followers on Twitter. If your faker number runs under 20-percent, you tend to be on the safe side. On TwitterCounter.com, there is the option to enter the name and receive a three-month view of the follower count. If there are irregular significant jumps, then all signs point to fake." (Zaki 2013)

While there is still no sure way to find out if you bought Facebook friends or Instagram followers, there are a few signs that employers look for:

Those in the medical and health care community have not been immune from social media ethics challenges.

According to an article in scrubsmag.com (Fink 2010), five nurses, who worked at Tri-City Medical Center in Oceanside, CA, lost their jobs because of Facebook posts, although the CEO of Tri-City Medical Center said no patient names, photos, or identifying information were included in the posts.

"In 2009, Wisconsin nurses were fired after two nurses took photos of a patient's X-ray and allegedly posted it to Facebook. While the Facebook page was quickly removed, one of the nurses in question admitted to discussing the incident on her Facebook page." (Fink 2010)

The questions remain as follows:

1. Should health care professionals be permitted to discuss patient care online?
2. Should health care professionals be permitted to show patient pictures?

Singapore Airlines stepped into the fray after posting what some considered to be unethical and insensitive posts about the downing of Malaysia Airlines Flight MH17 over Ukraine on July 17, 2014, killing all 283 passengers and 15 crew on board. "Right after the crash of MH17, Singapore took to Twitter and Facebook claiming that their planes do not fly across the Ukrainian airspace. The posts received hundreds of scathing comments in social media, from people saying that they were "unethical."" (Sison 2014)

Big brands in the United States have also found themselves embroiled in social media ethics controversies, including major designer and retailer Kenneth Cole. A tweet went out in 2013 that attempted to tie into

*Source:* Broderick, R. 2013. "Kenneth Cole Decided to Tweet Something Completely Stupid About Syria." Retrieved from http://www.buzzfeed.com/ryanhatesthis/kenneth-cole-decided-to-tweet-something-completely

war-torn Syria. The point here is how could such a respectable brand believe that a marketing pitch tied to "boots on the ground" would be acceptable? (Broderick 2013)

"An example of a questionably unethical social media practice would be after the Boston Marathon Bombing when NBC Bay Area posted a photo of a bombing victim and asked people to "Like" the photo to wish him a speedy recovery. This was an attempt to manipulate people's feelings for a young victim of the bombing in order to receive an edge in the social media rankings over other networks (Ray 2013)." (mediaethicsafternoon.wordpress.com 2014)

Businesses and organizations simply need to "think before they tweet." It's a matter of sensitivity.

As you may recall, on July 20, 2012, a mass shooting occurred inside of a movie theater in Aurora, Colorado, during a screening of the film *The Dark Knight Rises*. A gunman shot into the audience with multiple firearms, killing 12 people and injuring 70 others.

Shortly after the National Rifle Association (NRA) broadcast a tweet that was met with a substantial backlash in Colorado reading, "Good morning, shooters: Happy Friday! Weekend plans?" (Fitzpatrick 2012)

## Good morning, shooters. Happy Friday! Weekend plans?

*Source:* Fitzpatrick, A. 2012. "NRA Tweet." Retrieved from http://mashable.com/2012/07/20/nra-tweet/

The backlash was quick and vocal:

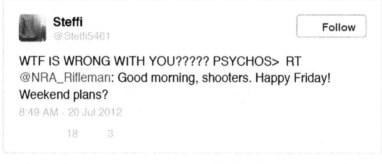

*Source:* Fitzpatrick, A. 2012. "NRA Tweet." Retrieved from http://mashable.com/2012/07/20/nra-tweet/

In 2012, Hurricane Sandy went on record as the second costliest hurricane in U.S. history, causing damage estimated at over $68 billion. What did The Gap do on Twitter? The company sent out this tweet: "All impacted by #Sandy, stay safe! We'll be doing lots of Gap.com shopping today. How about you?" (Wasserman 2012)

**Gap** ✔
@Gap

 Follow

All impacted by #Sandy, stay safe! We'll be doing lots of
Gap.com shopping today. How about you? 4sq.com/
QPVDT9

29/10/2012 14:32

**A check-in at Frankenstorm Apocalypse - Hurricane
Sandy**

Other Great Outdoors in New York, NY

Foursquare @foursquare

*Source*: Wasserman, T. 2012. "Gap Criticized for Insensitive Tweet During Hurricane Sandy."
Retrieved from http://mashable.com/2012/10/31/gap-tweet-hurricane-sandy/

Once again, there was a strong consumer backlash:

**jontando**
@jontando

👤▾  Follow

@Gap Try taking a break from being a shill
for a couple of days instead of trying to tie in
a life-threatening storm warning to your
ads?

← Reply   ⇄ Retweet   ★ Favorite

1            1
RETWEET   FAVORITE

*Source*: Wasserman, T. 2012. "Gap Criticized for Insensitive Tweet During Hurricane Sandy."
Retrieved from http://mashable.com/2012/10/31/gap-tweet-hurricane-sandy/

## Fake Reviews

The issue of fake reviews has also plagued Yelp and other sources. In fact,
some businesses have been caught offering to pay for fake reviews (which
is illegal) (Pinkham 2014).

*Source*: Pinkham, C.A. 2014. "Oh Look, a Company Is Paying People to Post Fake Yelp Reviews." Retrieved from http://kitchenette.jezebel.com/oh-look-a-company-is-paying-people-to-post-fake-yelp-r-1641909713

http://marketingland.com/yelp-sues-to-take-down-paid-review-mill-49953

What drives this unethical behavior? As we will see later in this chapter, **money**.

## Is It a "Review" or an Advertisement?

The problem goes much deeper than fake reviews or unethical tweets.

When you read a product or service review, or see someone's social media post extolling the virtues of a restaurant or product, you want that to come from someone who has purchased and used the product or service, not someone who is "hired" or paid with some other form of compensation to say nice things about the business. That is great in an ideal world, but we do not live in an ideal world, which is why the Federal

Trade Commission has issued important "guidelines" to all businesses, why prosecutors in some states have fined businesses for fake reviews, and why journalists have exposed some businesses for hiring people to post fake reviews.

A "testimonial," or a consumer review, must be from someone who has used the product or service, and/or believes in the brand or the cause, and writes honestly about it; otherwise, it's an "advertisement." **This means online reviews must be based on real experiences with the product, service, or venue.** If you write a fake review, encourage a fake review, or compensate anyone for a fake review, you are liable under Federal Trade Commission rules.

### Reviews vs. Advertising

Typically, in business, ***advertising is "paid,"*** which means that a business has usually provided some sort of compensation to either the person/group making the claim and providing the space for the claim (TV, Print, Radio, Internet, Social Media). An advertisement is usually a marketing message designed to persuade consumers to take action, whether it is to buy a product, use a service, vote for a political candidate or issue, and so on.

Now there is a category in which some people receive a form of "compensation: such as free concert tickets, free clothing or cosmetics for bloggers, products to test, free books to review, computers or electronics to review, cars to test drive, and so on." The Federal Trade Commission has said a business or organization can engage in these practices as long as the person receiving the goods discloses that clearly and conspicuously in their posts. In these cases, we need to know the reviewer has received the product for free to use and/or keep, and what they thought of it. If they do not reveal they have received some sort of compensation, we are left believing they love the product or service without the context that they were "paid" and it is not a true "testimonial."

We both can live with the fact that some expert electronics and computer journalists are given or allowed to test new computers and software, but we need to know that up front; the same holds true if we see a glowing review for a new car. But what if you see a great review for a book or a film? Does it make a difference whether the person works at the theater and saw the film for free, or was given the book for free? The answer is yes, and it should. You and I both need to know whether this was a genuine, unsolicited testimonial review, or prompted by the delivery of a free product or service. Then we have the context to make an educated decision.

In 2013, New York regulators announced a major crackdown on deceptive Internet reviews. According to the New York Times, the yearlong investigation fined 19 businesses for misleading practices and ordered them to pay of $350,000 in penalties." (Streitfeld 2013)

These fake reviews can damage lives. "The investigation uncovered a wide range of services buying fake reviews that could do more permanent damage: dentists, lawyers, even an ultrasound clinic." (Streitfeld 2013)

"Among those were a charter bus operator, a teeth-whitening service, and a laser hair-removal chain. There were also several reputation-enhancement firms that place fraudulent reviews on sites like Google, Yelp, Citysearch, and Yahoo." (Streitfeld 2013)

The challenge is that for many people, when you read a review on sites like Yelp, Yahoo, Google, and Citysearch, you think you are reading an authentic testimonial review—when it's not, that's deception.

## Why Fake Reviews?

Why? Money and consumer eyeballs. Seventy-one percent of people read consumer reviews before making a purchase, according to a study conducted by Bazaarvoice, a company that helps companies and brands with authentic consumer-generated content. The study also found that seven out of 10 U.S. consumers have questioned the trustworthiness of reviews across the web (Miller 2015).

How does this happen? In some cases, friends of business owners do it, while in other cases, people are hired by businesses to write fake reviews.

Why do they do it? It means business. ***Money.***

As I mentioned earlier in this book, reviews, testimonials, and word of mouth recommendations have become more trusted than traditional advertising.

"Eight-five-percent of fans of brands on Facebook recommend brands to others." (syncapse.com 2013)

"Seventy-two-percent say reading a positive customer review increases their trust in the business; it takes reading between 2-6 reviews to get 56-percent of them to this point." (BrightLocal.com 2014)

"Studies show even the smallest push for fake positive reviews makes a huge difference in restaurant success. According to a University of California, Berkeley study, a slight half-star improvement increases the number of dinner reservations at an eatery." (Pan 2012)

"Third-party businesses are getting rich busting out five-star reviews. Entrepreneurs offer to write positive restaurant reviews on help-for-hire sites like Fiverr and online forum Digital Point, according to *The New York Times*." (Pan 2012)

## What's A Star Worth?

A study by Harvard Business School assistant professor Michael Luca concluded that ". . . a positive evaluation on Yelp.com does, in fact, appear to lead to increased business for restaurants. "Reviews, Reputation and Revenue: The Case of Yelp.com," analyzes review data from both Yelp and all Seattle restaurants from 2003 to 2009, and draws three conclusions about the Yelp effect on restaurants:"

1. A one-star increase in Yelp rating leads to a 5 to 9 percent increase in revenue.
2. This effect is driven by independent restaurants; ratings do not affect restaurants with chain affiliation.
3. Chain restaurants have declined in market share as Yelp penetration has increased. (Harvardmagazine.com 2011)

## The Problem is Growing

By now, you must be thinking this is still a small problem: Not so.

"A 2012 Gartner study estimated that one in seven recommendations or ratings on social media sites like Facebook would soon be fake. And there have been instances where all the reviews of a product have been secretly bought and paid for by the seller of the product." (Streitfeld 2013)

Gartner Inc., the world's leading information technology research and advisory company, predicted that by the start of 2015, 10 to 15 percent of social media reviews would be fakes, paid for by businesses. (gartner.com 2012)

According to Review Trackers, 21 percent of Americans have written a review for a product or service they never used. "The fake review problem exists in the first place because the marketing potential of reviews is just huge," says Chris Campbell, chief executive and founder of Review Trackers, a service that helps businesses aggregate and manage online reviews . "Business owners have thus seen it fit to try and game the system, and they pay hired review writers to pose as happy customers in order to improve their business reputation." (Fuscaldo 2014)

"With over half of the Internet's population on social networks, organizations are scrambling for new ways to build bigger follower bases, generate more hits on videos, garner more positive reviews than their competitors and solicit 'likes' on their Facebook pages," said Jenny Sussin, senior research analyst at Gartner. "Many marketers have turned to paying for positive reviews with cash, coupons and promotions including additional hits on YouTube videos in order to pique site visitors' interests in the hope of increasing sales, customer loyalty and customer advocacy through social media 'word of mouth' campaigns." (gartner.com 2012)

"Organizations engaging in social media can help to promote trust by openly embracing both positive and negative reviews and leveraging negative reviews as a way to encourage customers with positive product or service experiences to share them on review sites as well," Ms. Sussin said. "They should also respond to ratings and reviews in an official capacity to demonstrate willingness to engage in productive conversation with anyone." (gartner.com 2012)

### Amazon.com Cracks Down

In October 2015, Amazon sued more than 1,000 sellers of phony product reviews, for misleading Amazon's customers "by selling" fake reviews of products." This came after Amazon sued several websites earlier in 2015 for selling false reviews. (Miller 2015) The lawsuit targeted account holders on Fiverr.com, a marketplace for odd-jobs where work opportunities are sold for $5 and up." (Wattles 2015)

## Can Fake Reviews Lead to Skepticism by Consumers?

The answer may well be yes. Fake reviews and testimonials may be back-firing in more ways than one. They may lead to a loss of trust by the public, and this would be tragic.

"A survey about attitudes to online marketing techniques, such as fake Facebook 'likes', tweets about brands, and hiding negative reviews from search engine results, suggests that marketers are a lot more relaxed about such practices than the public." (Gallivan 2014)

"The survey, conducted among 3,000 consumers and 1,000 marketers in the U.K. by pollster YouGov PLC for the Chartered Institute of Marketing, found that 67-percent of consumers think techniques to hide negative content within search results are unethical, against just 38-percent of marketers." And consumers are also more scathing about companies giving products away to encourage positive reviews online, with only 48-percent thinking the practice is acceptable, compared with 66-percent of marketers." (blogs.wsj.com 2014)

## Can Consumers Trust Online Reviews?

The logical question is whether you can trust consumer reviews? The answer is "Yes But.." yes, but read carefully and be mindful of the source. For instance, if you are reading reviews for a relatively new restaurant, your "review red flags" should go up when you see all five stars the first week for a restaurant that has only been open for two weeks.

Whether it is a restaurant or hotel, there are real consumers and honest business operators, and then there are the, well, unscrupulous.

"Researchers at Yale, Dartmouth, and USC found evidence that hotel owners post fake reviews to boost their ratings on the site—and might even be posting negative reviews of nearby competitors." (Fisman 2012)

"One **widely reported study** showed that a text-analysis algorithm proved remarkably adept at detecting made-up reviews. The researchers instructed freelance writers to put themselves in the role of a hotel marketer who has been tasked by his boss with writing a fake customer review that is flattering to the hotel. They also compiled a set of comparison TripAdvisor reviews that the study's authors felt were likely to be genuine.

Human judges could not distinguish between the real ones and the fakes. But the algorithm correctly identified the reviews as real or phony with 90-percent accuracy by picking up on subtle differences, like whether the review described specific aspects of the hotel room layout (the real ones do) or mentioned matters that were unrelated to the hotel itself, like whether the reviewer was there on vacation or business (a marker of fakes). Great, but in the cat-and-mouse game of fraud vs. fraud detection, phony reviewers can now design feedback that won't set off any alarm bells." (Fisman 2012)

## Dine and Duped!

This is a phrased I coined after I fell victim (like many of you) to some wonderful reviews about a restaurant. "Oh, the food is so wonderful." "The atmosphere is great." You get so much food." The reviews went on and on. What did I find? A $9 Caesar salad with a wedge of lettuce so small I needed a microscope to see it; two bites and the salad is history! I thought to myself, so much for those, uh, "fake" reviews.

## How Do You Spot a Fake Review?

This is a question I have not only asked myself as I read reviews, but one I have been asked hundreds of times.

In 2014, Mashable.com published a very helpful story that included several tips to help all of us look for "clues" about the reliability of reviews:

1. The reviewer has not reviewed anything else. Some consumers may like or hate a particular product or service so much that they feel compelled to write a single online review. However, one extremely positive or negative comment by a reviewer who has never reviewed anything else could be a red flag. Make sure to note the username and click to see his or her history.

2. The reviewer posts multiple reviews with similar language. If one reviewer has commented on multiple hotel listings with reviews that all sound eerily similar to one another, your instincts should be on high alert. This could be a clear sign of someone who is getting paid per review (and is being pretty lazy about hiding it).

3. The reviewer's language is oddly specific. Let us say you are reading a review for a product that has a really long name, like the "DEFG HydraHelix Smartwatch 2000x Chrome." Most reviewers are not going to write out the whole name multiple times, and will instead shorten it to something like the "HydraHelix." Fake reviewers will go all out, stating the full name as often as possible, because it juices up SEO points for the product.

4. Too Much Enthusiasm! If there is a lot of excessive punctuation and overly positive language, put on your skeptical specs.

5. A hotel review that focuses too much on family and activities. A 2013 study by Cornell University found that fake hotel reviewers would often emphasize all the great activities and family fun the place provides, whereas real reviewers focused mostly on the hotel itself. It is a ploy to make a review sound as personal and relatable as possible. Plus, it is a way for the reviewer, who is likely never stepped foot in that hotel, to avoid writing details about the hotel itself.

To combat fake reviews, here are some nearly foolproof ways to determine if a comment is legitimate:

- Verified reviews: Some sites have a means of verifying reviewers. For example, Amazon marks whether or not a reviewer actually purchased a reviewed item from the online store.
- Social media accounts: Some sites require reviewers to post comments by using their Facebook account. Thus, it puts a face to the comment. You can always click on that person's account and check out the profile to see how "real" he or she is.
- If you're hunting for hotels, try Review Skeptic, a beta site based on research from Cornell University. Copy and paste reviews onto the site's homepage and it will let you know if they are real or fake, based on language analysis. (Desta 2014)

FOX Business reporter Donna Fuscaldo also provides some advice in her 2014 article about how to spot the "fakes" from the real reviews:

**Fraud Alert No. 1: Too Good to Be True**: Nobody is perfect, and a company, product, or service with nothing but five-star reviews should cause consumers to pause. "If all you see is five stars, you got to start suspecting these guys work for the manufacturer," says Udi Ledergor, chief executive of online review company Yotpo. "Even when you are happy with a product there are usually some negatives."

**Fraud Alert No. 2: Product Feature Reviews**: Emotion is a main part of the buying process, which means it should also show up in reviews. According to Campbell, real reviewers will talk about the value and performance of the product or service instead of solely focusing on the features. What's more, he says real review writers typically include information about how they used the product and how it worked. Reviews that only list the features with no emotion or interaction with it tend to be fake, he says.

**Fraud Alert No. 3: Language in Review is Exact and Not Every Day**: Authors of fake reviews want their review to show up high in search results, which is why they will make a point of using the exact product name and model numerous times through a review. They also tend to use words the average person would not, such as "explosive speed" or "revolutionary cutting-edge technology," says Campbell. "No one talks like that, so it's reasonable to expect the review to be fake," he says.

**Fraud Alert No. 4: Too Polished Pictures**: They say a picture is worth 1,000 words, and when it comes to the legitimacy of a review, an overly-polished image or one that is found all over the Internet could signal a counterfeit review.

"Consumers often focus on the review text, but accompanying photos and videos can also reveal which reviews could be fake," says Campbell. "If the pictures look too professional, or if a Google image search produces results for the same photos in various review sites, then it's more likely that the review is fake." (Fuscaldo 2014)

## Summary

In this chapter, we learned about poor social media ethics examples. We also learned why businesses hire people to submit fake reviews, how the problem is growing, what some companies are doing to stop fake reviews, and how to spot a fake review.

# CHAPTER 5

# Why We Need Ethics Policies and Guidelines

Before I discuss the Federal Trade Commission guidelines on disclosure and share how to create a social media ethics policy, it is important to review some of the mistakes people and businesses have made to fully understand the scope of the problem.

Sharlyn Lauby (2012) wrote an interesting article in American Express Open Forum about this very topic. She poses the following interesting questions we should all be asking ourselves:

"Both ethics and social media are important in the workplace, so the question becomes: What is the best way to manage them? Should they be treated as two distinct conversations? Or should ethics be addressed in social media policies?" (Lauby 2012)

Kristen Fyfe, senior communications manager at the Training and Development Association (ASTD), points out the component that both ethics and social media must have in common to be successful "Clarity is the most effective element for both ethics and social media policies, "Companies that have not incorporated behavior expectations into their employee handbooks should make that a top priority." (Lauby 2012)

**It's about setting clear expectations for your employees, volunteers, board members, and vendors.**

"If you identify yourself as a member of a company or organization, you are always on stage. Act like it. How you respond online will have as much or more resonance than in person, so either be on your best behavior or don't act as a brand advocate." (Lauby 2012)

Here is a question for you to think about: Do you think it is ethical for employers to consider what you have posted on your social media accounts in the hiring process?

I ask this because more employers are now using social media profiles in the hiring process.

"According to a survey from CareerBuilder, more than half of all employers (51-percent) who use social media for background information on potential employees are finding things that cause them to NOT hire the candidate." (TLNT.com 2014)

So, just what was it that employers are finding on social media sites that makes them decide to pass on a job candidate? CareerBuilder listed the most common ones:

- Job candidate posted provocative or inappropriate photographs or information—46 percent
- Job candidate posted information about them drinking or using drugs—41 percent
- Job candidates bad-mouthed their previous company or fellow employee—36 percent
- Job candidate showed poor communication skills—32 percent
- Job candidate posted discriminatory comments related to race, gender, religion, and others—28 percent
- Job candidate lied about qualifications—25 percent
- Job candidate shared confidential information from previous employers—24 percent
- Job candidate was linked to criminal behavior—22 percent
- Job candidate's screen name was unprofessional—21 percent
- Job candidate lied about an absence—13 percent

(TLNT.com 2014)

There is a downside to using social media posts in the screening process for job applicants.

It is perceived as sneaky. People change and grow. A comment posted to an article last year may or may not reflect the person's attitude this year. You might learn things you really do not want to know such as age, religious affiliation, marital status, medical history, caregiving status, and so on. (Spraggins 2014)

Will Stoughton, a doctoral student in industrial psychology and lead author on a study about how job candidates perceive employers who snoop at work is quoted as saying, "The practice may have serious repercussions for the hiring organization's reputation and make applicants more inclined to resort to litigation." That is because job seekers view online searches as an invasion of privacy. But perhaps the most compelling reason to not view online profiles is that whatever the employer finds may not be predictive of an individual's job performance. (Spraggins 2014)

Some insurance companies are also using social media posts, which raises the question once again: Is it ethical to use our posts in determining insurance rates? To be fair, insurance companies are not big, bad meanies who are out to prevent people from getting insurance or to gouge a policyholder with high rates. Instead, they are working to lessen their risk. Nevertheless, does our private life have any bearing on what we should be charged by insurance companies?

Underwriters are looking for things making you higher risk, noting possible habits you seem to enjoy, as well as your medical history. For example, smoking, drinking, or even leading a sedentary lifestyle makes you more vulnerable to serious health issues. Case in point—the classic "smoker question." If you check "no" to being a smoker on your life insurance application, but yet you have a cigarette in your hand in every photo of you online, and you "Like" and "Follow" the Marlboro Man, it is a safe bet that one, you are a smoker, and/or two, you are either still doing or have done considerable damage to your body and increased your risks of cancer and heart disease. Health insurers may deny benefits completely, deny claims, or even cancel coverage mid-policy (insurancequotes.org 2014).

Sometimes what people share via social media stops things from even getting too far. Consider the case of Jacob Cox-Brown from Astoria, Oregon. Police were perplexed on January 1, 2013, as to who may have sideswiped two cars during the night. It did not take long to figure it out. A message was sent to an officer with Cox-Brown's status update: "*Drivin drunk. . . classic but to whoever's vehicle I hit I am sorry. :P*" After police arrived at his house and matched the damage to his car, Cox-Brown was arrested.

Cox-Brown now claims it was all "a big joke." To insurance companies though, this type of situation is no laughing matter. Had Cox-Brown not given himself away, he could have easily submitted a hit and run claim with his insurance company and possibly received benefits—which would have been a fraudulent claim. (insurancequotes.org 2014)

In addition to higher premiums, there are denied claims. In Canada, 29-year-old Natalie Blanchard was denied health benefits due to her Facebook posts. She was on long-term sick leave from her company due to major depression when her benefits were abruptly cut off. She called the insurer, Manulife, to question the stop payment. The insurance company informed her that since she had recently posted pictures of herself seemingly having good times at the bar, and sunning on the beach, she evidently was not depressed. Blanchard argued that she was going out on doctor's orders, in an attempt to "forget her problems." Maybe if her doctor had diagnosed her with seasonal affective disorder, it would have been another story—and, if her prescription had included bikinis and tall fruity drinks. Although Manulife made no comment on the specific incident, it positively confirmed that they, and other insurers, use social media to investigate clients. The company did say, "We would not deny or terminate a valid claim solely based on information published on websites such as Facebook." (insurancequotes.org 2014)

One group of workers that is always on stage is physicians. We hold them in high respect and count on them to uphold the highest ethics.

For physicians and for patients, the issue of relationships can be challenged by social media. Physicians want meaningful, professional relationships with patients. Patients want to know about their physicians and have trusting relationships with them. Enter social media. Doctors now face questions about how to use social media platforms such as Facebook and Twitter, even for their own private use.

Kevin O'Reilly addressed this issue head-on in an article published on amednews.com (American Medical News 2010), saying, "there is little professional guidance to help physicians navigate connections with patients on Facebook, Twitter and other sites. Some hospitals and medical schools have policies to direct physicians, medical students and other health professionals on how to use social media properly, but formal ethical guidance to help physicians maintain professional standards online is scarce. Doctors are largely on their own to devise rules on how to maintain appropriate boundaries with patients on social media." (American Medical News 2010)

The American College of Physicians' Center for Ethics and Professionalism is collaborating with the organization's Council of Associates, which represents more than 19,000 internal medicine residents and fellows, to formulate a social media policy to include in a revised ethics manual (American Medical News 2010).

## Over sharing?

Some doctors in training, have been guilty of over sharing. More than 60 percent of U.S. medical schools reported incidents of students posting unprofessional content such as photos showing inebriation or illegal drug use, or posts featuring vulgar language, according to a study in September 23/30, 2009, *Journal of the American Medical Association* (*JAMA*). Experts said such online disclosures can undermine patients' trust, and a physician's obligation to never violate patients' privacy continues to be paramount online.

However, subtler dilemmas such as whether to accept patients' Facebook friend requests are more common, because physicians see an opportunity to use social media to advance their patients' health. (American Medical News 2010)

At the same time, medical boards are now monitoring physician use of social media platforms (American Medical Association 2013).

When doctors go to social media websites, they may want to think twice about posting patients' photos without permission. Using the images could be considered unprofessional conduct by a state medical board, according to a new study. Other online physician behavior viewed as troublesome by boards: citing misleading information about clinical outcomes; misrepresenting credentials; and inappropriately contacting patients. (AMA 2014)

A survey of 48 state medical board executives, published in the *Annals of Internal Medicine*, found that these social media activities likely would prompt a board investigation of a doctor. The study concluded that physicians should never engage in such behaviors. "People can really do a lot to stay out of trouble by applying common sense and avoiding the trap that you can do something online you wouldn't do in real life," said study lead author Ryan Greysen, MD, MHS. He is an assistant professor in the Division of Hospital Medicine at the University of California, San Francisco, School of Medicine (AMA 2013).

Previous research has shown that doctors and medical students can get in trouble online. An article cowritten by Dr. Greysen in the March 21, 2012, issue of *JAMA* found that 71 percent of state medical boards had investigated doctors for violating professionalism online. A study, also cowritten by Dr. Greysen, on September 23, 2009, issue of *JAMA* said 60 percent of medical schools had incidents of students posting unprofessional content online. (AMA 2013)

## You Are What You Post: No Hiding from Fraud

We live in a world where many people share things they should not, from embarrassing photos to fraudulent behavior. Yes, I said fraud. And these posts are now the fraud investigator's best friend.

James Quiggle, Coalition against Insurance Fraud says, "Mining social media for clues is one of the fastest-growing areas of insurance-fraud investigation. For example, worker's compensation investigators might find that a supposedly injured employee is bragging about hang gliding and is posting action photos on Facebook." (Goldmann 2012)

According to Jaclyn S. Millner, an attorney at Fitch, Johnson, Larson & Held, P.A. and Gregory M. Duhl, Associate Professor of Law at the William Mitchell College of Law in St. Paul, Minnesota, there is nothing unethical or illegal about a defense attorney or an agent of the attorney, such as a company representative or investigator, accessing a fraud suspect's information and photographs that are stored on a social networking site and are not protected with privacy settings preventing public access. In that sense, according to the Millner and Duhl—who have researched and written extensively on the topic—searching for public information on a social networking site is no different than video surveillance in any public location that defense counsel may authorize in a fraud investigation (Goldmann 2012).

## Deception Matters

States differ on whether lawyers and their agents, including investigators and other company representatives, can engage in deception in investigations under the supervision of an attorney. In some states, for example, deceptive practices could technically include "friending" a fraud suspect under a false name or account in order to gain access to his or her private social networking account (Goldmann 2012).

## Teachers and Social Media: Crossing the Line?

Teachers spend their lives dedicated to students, working long hours, frequently for much lower pay than they might earn in other positions. With such an educated group, ethical questions arise:

1. Should teachers allow "friending" by students?
2. They must be mindful about posting comments about their peers, students, schools, and/or the education system.
3. They must not "vent" about their frustrations in the classrooms in online forums.

Unfortunately, that hasn't stopped some teachers from crossing the line.

The following should be lessons to be learned. They come from jobs. aol.com:

## Think You're Hot? Don't Tweet It!

I have been amazed at how some people, even in some of the most responsible positions, have made egregious errors of judgment when it comes to what they post on social media. From politicians to business people to teachers, it's critical to "think before you tweet." I share these stories to help remind you to share them with friends and family. Be a coach, be a mentor, help others avoid the mistakes these people made.

A 23-year-old high school math teacher in Aurora, Colorado, had a perfectly nice job until her superiors got wind of racy tweets. They included topless and other revealing self-portraits and messages like "stay sexy . . . stay high . . . stay drunk," to say nothing of referring to a student as "jail bait" or saying that she was high while grading papers. The teacher claimed that the Twitter account was a parody that she set up with friends. Students rallied to her defense. School administrators were not laughing when they first put her on paid administrative leave and then fired her. (Sherman 2013)

## Keep Your Side Career off Facebook

Having active outside interests helps teachers relax and stay in fine form. In the case of a part-time bikini model who taught English at a high school in Florida, it was literally true. One day, the principal called her into his office, showed some of her posing work on a computer screen, and asked if it was her. She said yes and he said good-bye (Sherman 2013).

## Don't Post Jokes About Wishing Your Students Would Drown

Teaching grade school can be challenging. But calling your fifth-grade students "devils spawn" that you would like to bring to the beach—the day after a sixth grader in Harlem had drowned in the ocean on a school outing—is completely inappropriate. That is what one teacher did in 2010, posting the rant on Facebook and then trying to cover up when officials heard about the vent. She was fired, although finally won a court battle to be reinstated. However, the 2-year suspension without pay was upheld, meaning her financial life likely remains underwater (Sherman 2013).

## Don't Post Photos of Your Students' Mouths Covered with Duct Tape

A middle school math teacher at a Community Learning Center in Ohio, thought posting a picture to Facebook of 16 students with duct tape on their mouths and a caption of "Finally found a way to keep them quiet!!!" was funny, particularly as she claims that the students had put the tape on themselves as a joke. She eventually realized that the post was a "huge mistake." Neither was the local board of education when it fired her (Sherman 2013).

## Don't Advise Students in A Religious Education Class to Sleep Around

Just to show that not all online nuttiness by teachers is restricted to the United States, a religious education teacher in England, allegedly told students to "sleep around" before marriage, swore in the classroom, and described some of her personal experiences concerning sex. And then, after a parents' night, she supposedly posted on Facebook, "That was the most ****** horrendous evening of my life." The 27-year-old reportedly was banned from classrooms for 5 years. (Sherman 2013)

What is missing? Social media polices that help teachers (and others) understand what is appropriate and inappropriate use of social media.

Who else needs to have a social media policy? Maybe sports franchises? Ayesha Curry, wife of Stephen Curry of the Golden State Warriors, took to Twitter June 16, 2016, after her husband was ejected from Game 6 for throwing his mouthpiece, which hit one of the Cavaliers' minority owners' sons. "I've lost all respect sorry this is absolutely rigged for money … Or ratings [I'm] not sure which. I won't be silent." She later deleted the tweet, which was mocked on social media. (usmagazine.com 2016)

## Gross, Disgusting, and What? No Social Media Policy?

You would think after so many videos and pictures have surfaced that frustrated employees of fast food restaurants would stop venting on social media, but you would be wrong. From restaurant workers to airline employees to others, some people think they can record unethical behavior on video or images, post it, and nothing will happen.

An image was shared on social media (Broderick 2013) of a Taco Bell employee licking a stack of taco shells.

A Denver math teacher tweets about her hot students and how she likes to smoke weed. Her students thought her racy photos and tweets about marijuana and club music were pretty cool, though, and protested online to get her back. She was fired in the end.

Former California Pizza Kitchen server and social media butterfly "Timothy DeLaGhetto" claimed he was fired for tweeting about how he did not like the company's new uniforms. As he explained in a since-deleted tweet to its corporate Twitter account, "black button ups are the lamest s--t ever!!!" (Broderick 2013)

## "Cisco Fatty" Takes On Twitter

You may also recall the case of a man who has come to be called "Cisco Fatty" after a social media mistake. After interviewing at Cisco Systems, even before starting his new job, this guy tweeted: "Cisco just offered me a job! Now I have to weigh the utility of a fatty paycheck against the daily commute to San Jose and hating the work."

"A channel partner advocate for Cisco Alert found the tweet and replied: "Who is the hiring manager. I'm sure they would love to know that you will hate the work. We here at Cisco are versed in the web." This unfortunate incident led to the man becoming known as "Cisco Fatty." What a reputation! (Huhman 2013)

What is missing? Social media polices that help people understand what is appropriate and inappropriate use of social media.

## Facebook Posts Tied to College Admissions?

While more than 80 percent of colleges use Facebook to recruit students, according to a Kaplan survey of college admissions officers, roughly a quarter of admissions officers are also stopping to check out the profiles of prospective students. Although this does not necessarily mean that Facebook and other online profiles will be considered in making admissions decisions, AllFacebook reports that at least one Harvard admissions officer—who posted on a Quora thread in response to the question "Do high school students' Facebook profiles affect their college applications?"—said that a student's online presence "absolutely" prejudices her." (HuffingtonPost.com 2011)

Over-sharing or deciding whether your profile on social media compromises your professionalism is just one part of this complicated issue. There are other aspects of ethics that happen when you pay someone to blog for you.

## Ghost Blogging

According to Blogossary, a ghost blog is a blog written and managed by an anonymous author(s). A ghost blog can also be a blog written by a person or company on behalf of another company or person (ethicsinpr. wikispaces.com n.d.).

According to opponents of ghost blogging, these practices constitute bloggers' ethics. Blogs that do not follow these practices are therefore unethical and threaten the integrity of the medium. Those that are in favor of ghost blogging are adamant that the practice can be beneficial to both the company as well as the public as long as the writer and the corporation are sharing the same viewpoints and values. Another argument in favor of ghost blogging mentions the fact that public relations practitioners have always written speeches and news reports for others, so there should not be much difference between those practices and corporate ghost blogging. One of the main arguments against ghost blogging is the lack of transparency it provides for its audiences. Blogs are meant to add a human touch to an organization, so they should be constructed by someone who is situated within the corporation. A second argument against ghost blogging relates to the idea that social media is centered on creating connections between the writers and their audiences, a practice that does not generally account for any third-party mediation (ethicsinpr. wikispaces.com n.d.).

## Courtrooms, Cases, and Social Media

Today, everyone from prosecutors, to defense attorneys, to people involved in cases are also engaging in social media practices, bringing into question whether social media policies are needed.

The extent of the problem goes beyond those in the legal profession. Even the families of both defendants and victims are now creating Facebook pages about cases; gang members have taken to social media in an attempt to menace witnesses; and journalists are tweeting and texting from courtrooms during trials. The use of social media in court is becoming increasingly prevalent (BWGlaw.net 2014).

Courts around the country are working hard to update their policies on using social media in the courtroom. A Tucson attorney and jury consultant, Rosalind Greene, writes about the usage of social media in the courtroom. She recently discussed a study that found that, between 1999 and 2010, at least 90 verdicts were appealed across the country because of Internet or social media gaffes, 28 of those were overturned, and half of those appeals happened in 2009 and 2010 (BWGlaw.net 2014).

Researchers monitoring Twitter found that people who identified themselves as prospective or sitting jurors tweeted every three minutes (BWGlaw.net 2014).

## Are You Kidding?

In Britain, a juror took to social media to ask if she should find a defendant guilty or not guilty.

A mistrial was declared after five members of a Baltimore jury "friended" each other on Facebook during a political corruption trial and discussed the case online.

A judge in New York State was disciplined for becoming "friends" with lawyers on social media.

A federal judge in New Jersey had doubts about the testimony of a witness, so she went on Facebook to check out that witness.

A Michigan juror posted an inappropriate post to her Facebook page, which read: "Gonna be fun to tell the defendant they're GUILTY." (BWGlaw.net 2014)

## Social Media Posts Admissible in Court

Yes, and in divorce cases too!

A survey from Lawyers.com shows that only 46 percent of Facebook users realize their posts can be used as legal evidence. Users of other social media sites were even less aware; 44 percent of YouTube users, 38 percent of Twitter users, 32 percent of Instagram users, and 25 percent of Vine users understood that their activity can come back to bite them. The survey results show that users under 24 are about twice as likely to be aware that their posts can be used against them as users who are 55 or older. Users with lower household incomes and educational levels were also less likely to expect their online lives to come up in court than their wealthier, degree-holding counterparts. (Crank 2013)

## What You Say On Facebook Can Be Used Against You in A Court of Law

Whether it is a divorce proceeding or criminal trial, posts on social networking sites such as Facebook, MySpace, Twitter, and Skype are regularly popping up as evidence in courtrooms locally and across the country (Callahan 2012).

Ian Friedman, past president of the Ohio Association of Criminal Defense Attorneys said, "I personally have been involved in several trials where credibility was completely lost in a matter of seconds when the witness was presented with something inconsistent they had written in the past." (Callahan 2012)

The Internet website Forensic Focus posted a study by a lawyer who pulled up almost 700 appeals cases, nationwide, where social media was at least part of the disagreement over a trial court outcome. John Patzakis, the study's author, wrote the cases he was able to locate are likely just the tip of the iceberg—since only a small percentage of all appellate decisions are published online. And he estimates "several, if not tens of thousands," of cases involving social media are out there. That fact worries Ohio Supreme Court Justice Judith Lanzinger, who once said courts are in the "wild, wild west" in terms of dealing with new technology. Lanzinger said the court needs to find ways to deal with emerging technology, particularly with the ability to doctor photos and create fake accounts on some social networking platforms (Callahan 2012).

## Child Custody, Family Court, Social Media, and Ethics

Over the last few years, we have seen more social media sites used in family law cases, which brings into question whether there should be ethics policies regarding the use of this content. Should it be kept private or is it evidence being used for the welfare of children?

How can social media content be used in this context? Posts may be used as evidence to demonstrate a person's spending habits, behavior, personal relationships, purchases made, job skills, partying, anger issues, use of alcohol or drugs, and so on.

The experts at Maley Investigations and Detective Agency in Libertyville, Illinois point out that, "A major aspect of a child custody dispute is the safety of the child and a parent's lifestyle affects the child's well-being. How you conduct yourself on social media websites can hurt your case. The best thing you can do if you are in the middle of a nasty custody battle is refrain from using social media websites entirely. If you post any material that is questionable, then rest assured your ex-spouse will retrieve it and try to use it against you in court." (maleyinvestigations.com 2014)

Here are some real-life scenarios that were used against a person in a divorce/child custody case: (maleyinvestigations.com 2014)

1. The husband joined Match.com and declared he was single and childless, while he was seeking primary custody of his children.
2. A husband denied he had any anger management issues, but still posted on Facebook, "If you have the balls to get in my face, I'll kick your ass into submission."
3. A wife was fighting for custody of her children while evidence surfaced from the gaming site "World of Warcraft" tracked her online and chatting with her boyfriend at the precise time she claimed to be out with her children.
4. A mother denied in court that she smoked marijuana, but posted pictures on Facebook of her smoking marijuana.
5. A soon-to-be ex-husband claimed he was unemployed, and he was receiving temporary alimony payments from his wife. However, on Facebook, the unemployed man described himself as a business owner and he also wrote details about trips to Las Vegas, South America, and to Sea World, all taken with his new girlfriend. At the divorce trial, the judge denied the husband's request to receive any type of alimony.
6. A father claimed he could not afford to pay any type of child support. However, his online postings showed off photographs of him sitting in a Ferrari, taking a cruise, and selling land that he owned.

## Should Jurors Have a Social Media Ethics Policy?

Some of the cases have been under the radar but others have been high profile.

During the 2009 trial of former Pennsylvania State Sen. Vincent Fumo, a television station covering the trial discovered that one of the jurors had repeatedly posted about the case on Facebook and Twitter (Hall 2014).

Other issues?

A post announcing that a person was selected for a jury, or complaining that he or she will miss a week of work can invite a response that might subtly influence a juror's view of the case (Hall 2014).

Example Post: "Jury duty 2morrow. I may get 2 hang someone . . . can't wait." (The juror, who was not identified, posted on his Facebook wall (Hall 2014).

The potential for social media to influence a juror is significant, says criminal defense attorney Gerald Grimaud, a member of the Civil and Equal Rights Committee of the Pennsylvania Bar Association (Hall 2014).

## The Bottom Line

Anything that you post to a social media account may be used against you in court. In August 2012, U.S. District Judge William Pauley III ruled that posts on Facebook are admissible in court, even if your profile is not public. If you have a high privacy setting, your social media posts may be admissible in court if one of your "friends" shares them with government officials or the court (drewcochranlaw.com 2014).

In addition, "When you post a comment on someone else's social media profile page, or "wall," that results in damages, a judge may find you liable. For example, if a woman gets hired to work as a nanny for the summer and a vengeful ex-friend posts a harmful lie on the woman's social media wall that results in her getting fired, a judge may order the ex-friend to pay the would-be nanny the amount of money that she would have earned during the summer. At the same time, the ex-friend may have to admit to her malintent or the parent may have to testify that the post influenced the hiring decision (drewcochranlaw.com 2014).

Regardless of the platform, social media is never private. There is always a way to access posts, even if you think you have deleted content from your profile. The best way to prevent having your social media posts used against you in court is to post comments and pictures that do not compromise your integrity. In addition, you can keep others from posting pictures or messages about you by changing your privacy settings. Instead of deleting posts from your social media accounts during legal proceedings, talk to your lawyer about the best way to do damage control legally (drewcochranlaw.com 2014).

# Summary

In this chapter, we have seen a myriad of examples of unethical behavior. It is important to understand the scope of this behavior to better understand why social media ethics policies are needed.

We have also seen how some businesses and organizations, from insurance companies to higher education, are now looking at social media posts and using content as criteria for acceptance. The question is whether you consider this to be ethical.

# CHAPTER 6

# The Federal Trade Commission Steps In

The Federal Trade Commission (FTC) has given you a gift. When was the last time a government agency gave you a gift? Now this gift does not come in a wrapped package with a ribbon, but it is just as valuable because it could protect your reputation, your job, and the reputation of your business or organization.

First, let us start with a message from the FTC.

In an effort to avoid deceptive practices, the FTC issued important "guidelines" regarding disclosure, primarily related to online advertising. These guidelines were updated in 2011 and again in 2013, renaming it *.com Disclosures: How to Make Effective Disclosures in Digital Advertising.* According to the FTC, "*.com Disclosures* focuses on the same consumer protection principles, but fast-forwards them to reflect changes in the digital marketplace."

In the online marketplace, consumers can transact business without the constraints of time or distance. One can log on to the Internet day or night and purchase almost anything one desires, and advances in mobile technology allow advertisers to reach consumers nearly anywhere they go. But cyberspace is not without boundaries, and deception is unlawful no matter what the medium. The FTC has enforced and will continue enforcing its consumer protection laws to ensure that products and services are described truthfully online, and that consumers understand what they are paying for. These activities benefit consumers as well as sellers, who expect and deserve the opportunity to compete in a marketplace free of deception and unfair practices (Federal Trade Commission 2013).

The general principles of advertising law apply online, but new issues arise almost as fast as technology develops—most recently, new issues have arisen concerning space-constrained screens and social media platforms (Federal Trade Commission 2013).

The same consumer protection laws that apply to commercial activities in other media apply online, including activities in the mobile marketplace. The FTC Act's prohibition on "unfair or deceptive acts or practices" encompasses online advertising, marketing, and sales. In addition, many Commission rules and guides are not limited to any particular medium used to disseminate claims or advertising, and therefore, apply to the wide spectrum of online activities (Federal Trade Commission 2013).

So there, you have it; ***the FTC has said that consumer protection laws apply to all forms of media, and this includes social media.***

## It's About Disclosure

The FTC guidelines address multiple areas of social media disclosure. While the report provides many specific details about disclosure requirements, the general theme is that organizations must consider the social medium, the technology used to access the information, the visibility of the disclosure, and the accessibility of the disclosure when crafting disclosure statements.

According to the FTC report, ***disclosures should be obvious, easily accessible, easily understood, and placed in a location that users would normally pay attention***. Disclosures should also be repeated if necessary and provided before a user purchases any good or service. The report gives specific guidance as what not to do when writing a disclosure. Absolutely do not include placing a disclosure at the end of a webpage, requiring users to click multiple times to get to the disclosure, or placing the disclosure in an inconspicuous place (Myers 2014).

## Disclosure Must Be Clear and Conspicuous

In the .com Disclosure document, the FTC has said that social media endorsements, testimonials, advertisements, and ads on social, digital and mobile media sites must be accompanied by ***clear and conspicuous disclosure*** to avoid deceptive practices.

According to the FTC, "It's the law—and it's always been the law—that if the disclosure of information is necessary to prevent an online ad claim from being deceptive or unfair, it has to be clear and conspicuous. So, what's new? According to *.com Disclosures* circa 2013, advertisers should make sure their disclosures are clear and conspicuous on all devices and platforms that consumers may use to view their ads. That means that if an ad would be deceptive or unfair (or would otherwise violate an FTC rule) without a disclosure—but the disclosure can't be made clearly and conspicuously on a particular device or platform—then that ad shouldn't run on that device or platform."

The new advice, according to *.com Disclosures: How to Make Effective Disclosures in Digital Advertising*, ". . .disclosures should be 'as close as possible' to the relevant claim. The new document calls on advertisers to label hyperlinks as specifically as possible. Another thing to bear in mind: how hyperlinks will function across the broad range of programs and devices consumers are likely to use."

Examining these new guidelines, four suggestions emerge for marketers: (Myers 2014)

1. Disclosures should be tailored to the structure of certain social media. Twitter disclosures are not the same as blog disclosures because of the structure of the sites.
2. Limited space in social media outlets does not mean an organization is absolved from providing complete disclosure information. If proper disclosures cannot be made in a particular social media outlet, then that site should not be used for promotional materials.
3. When drafting a disclosure, practitioners should think like ordinary social media users. Using jargon, providing information overload, or placing the disclosure in an obscure location that requires scrolling is not evidence of proper disclosure.
4. When writing a disclosure, practitioners should not only consider the limitation of a social media platform but also limitations of technological devices. Users read information in a variety of ways, including on tablets, smart phones, and traditional computers. Practitioners should consider the ordinary use of these and future

technologies and anticipate how ordinary users consume information on these devices.

But the disclosure requirement goes well beyond social media and digital "advertisements." It also applies to posts by everyone from employees, vendors, board members, and anyone with a vested interest in seeing a business succeed.

"In its simplest form, the disclosure requirement means that if you work for a business and you post why someone should buy a product, use the service, or go to the venue, you need to disclose that you work for that business or the relationship you have with that business." (Myers 2014)

## Disclosure Should Be "Clear and Conspicuous"

Andy Sernovitz, author of the book *Word of Mouth Marketing*, says disclosure can be as simple as *"I work for _____ and this is my personal opinion."*

I love how Andy has simplified disclosure to an easy, magical 10 words. These 10 words can keep you and your business on the safe side of the law. Put these into your policy, train your employees and stakeholders to use these words—relentlessly.

## Clear and Conspicuous

The FTC says the key is to make sure the disclosure is *"clear and conspicuous."* By comparison, you cannot put this disclosure at the bottom of your Facebook page, Twitter page, or your blog. *It needs to be associated with each post.*

This quote from the FTC should make the agency's intent perfectly clear: "Don't hide the ball." How many times does a government document use that kind of language? The FTC goes on to say that simply including a hyperlink may not be "clear and conspicuous" disclosure.

"Hyperlinks that simply say "disclaimer," "more information," "details," "terms and conditions," or "fine print" do not convey the importance, nature, and relevance of the information to which they lead and are likely to be inadequate. Even labels such as "important information" or "important limitations" may be inadequate." (Federal Trade Commission 2013)

Disclosures that are required to prevent an advertisement from being deceptive, unfair, or otherwise violative of a Commission rule, must be presented "clearly and conspicuously." Whether a disclosure meets this standard is measured by its performance; that is, how consumers actually perceive and understand the disclosure within the context of the entire ad. If a disclosure is not seen or comprehended, it will not change the net impression consumers take from the ad and therefore cannot qualify the claim to avoid a misleading impression (Federal Trade Commission 2013).

## Make it Obvious

Choosing the right label for the hyperlink. A hyperlink that leads to a disclosure should be labeled clearly and conspicuously.

Consumers should be able to tell that they can click on a hyperlink to get more information. Simply underlining text may be insufficient to inform consumers that the text is a hyperlink.

The FTC adds: "Don't be subtle. Symbols or icons by themselves are not likely to be effective as hyperlink labels leading to disclosures that are necessary to prevent deception." (Federal Trade Commission 2013)

Label the link to convey the importance, nature, and relevance of the information to which it leads. Example: The hyperlink should give consumers a reason to click on it. That is, the label should make clear that the link is related to a particular advertising claim or product and indicate the nature of the information to be found by clicking on it. The hyperlink label should use clear, understandable text (Federal Trade Commission 2013).

There is no set formula for a clear and conspicuous disclosure; it depends on the information that must be provided and the nature of the advertisement. Some disclosures are quite short, while others are more detailed. Some ads use only text, while others use graphics, video, or audio, or combinations thereof. Advertisers have the flexibility to be creative in designing their ads, as long as necessary information is communicated effectively and the overall message conveyed to consumers is not misleading ( Federal Trade Commission 2013).

## Technology Is Not an Excuse

The FTC addresses technology by telling businesses and organizations they must address these issues in disclosure, not avoid proper disclosure because of technology.

There are special considerations for evaluating whether a technique is appropriate for providing required disclosures. Do not ignore technological limitations. Some browsers or devices may not support certain techniques for displaying disclosures or may display them in a manner that makes them difficult to read. For example, a disclosure that requires Adobe Flash Player will not be displayed on certain mobile devices.

### Don't Use Blockable Pop-Up Disclosures

Advertisers should not disclose necessary information through the use of pop-ups that could be prevented from appearing by pop-up blocking software. Be aware of other issues with pop-up disclosures. Even the use of unblockable pop-ups to disclose necessary information may be problematic. Some consumers may not read information in pop-up windows or interstitials because they immediately close the pop-ups or move to the next page in pursuit of completing their intended tasks, or because they do not associate information in a pop-up window or on an interstitial page to a claim or product they have not encountered yet. However, advertisers can take steps to avoid such problems, for example, by requiring the consumer to take some affirmative action to proceed past the pop-up or interstitial (e.g., by requiring consumers to choose between yes and no buttons without use of preselected buttons before continuing). Research may be useful to help advertisers determine whether a particular technique is an effective method of communicating information to consumers (Federal Trade Commission 2013).

## Displaying Disclosures Prior to Purchase

Another important point according to the FTC is that ***disclosure must be made prior to purchase:***

Disclosures must be effectively communicated to consumers before they make a purchase or incur a financial obligation. In general, disclosures are more likely to be effective if they are provided in the context of the ad, when the consumer is considering the purchase. Where advertising and selling are combined on a website or mobile application—that is, the consumer will be completing the transaction online—disclosures should be provided before the consumer makes the decision to buy, for example, before clicking on an "order now" button or a link that says "add to shopping cart." (Federal Trade Commission 2013)

## Handling Short-Form Messages

The FTC has addressed the issue of short-form messaging, such as tweets, with very specific guidelines:

Use disclosures in each ad. If a disclosure is required in a space-constrained ad, such as a tweet, the disclosure should be in each and every ad that would require a disclosure if that ad was viewed in isolation. Do not assume that consumers will see and associate multiple space-constrained advertisements (Federal Trade Commission 2013).

Short-form disclosures might or might not adequately inform consumers of the essence of a required disclosure. For example, "Ad:" at the beginning of a tweet or similar short-form message should inform consumers that the message is an advertisement, and the word "Sponsored" likely informs consumers that the message was sponsored by an advertiser. Other abbreviations or icons may or may not be adequate, depending on whether they are presented clearly and conspicuously, and whether consumers understand their meaning so they are not misled. Misleading a significant minority of reasonable consumers is a violation of the FTC Act (Federal Trade Commission 2013).

Some disclosures can be placed at the beginning of a short-form message. Alternatively, if a disclosure is placed at the end of a message, the original message can be written with enough free space that the disclosure is not lost if the message is republished with a comment by others (Federal Trade Commission 2013).

## Watch for FTC Updates!

Although online commerce (including mobile and social media marketing) is booming, deception can dampen consumer confidence in the online marketplace. To ensure that products and services are described truthfully online and that consumers get what they pay for, the FTC will continue to enforce its consumer protection laws. Most of the general principles of advertising law apply to online ads, but new issues arise almost as fast as technology develops. The FTC will continue to evaluate online advertising, using traditional criteria, while recognizing the challenges that may be presented by future innovation. Businesses, as well, should consider these criteria when developing online ads and ensuring they comply with the law (Federal Trade Commission 2013)

Compliance with the FTC guide is voluntary; however, practices that are inconsistent with the FTC guide can be the basis of corrective action taken by the FTC, which could lead to fines—big fines!

## Summary

In this chapter, we have provided an overview of the Federal Trade Commission (FTC) social media disclosure guidelines. A business, organization, and/or individual must disclose its relationship to an ad or testimonial and that disclosure must be clear and conspicuous to the average consumer.

# CHAPTER 7

# How to Create a Social Media Policy

## What to Consider

Every business needs to have a social media policy to help guide staff and other stakeholders through the ethical standards your organization wants to uphold.

Did you fully understand that? Let me repeat it: According to the Federal Trade Commission, *"Every business needs to have a social media policy."*

Before doing so, it is important to think about what you want to accomplish and discuss some important questions.

Creating a social media ethics policy and guidelines should not be a year-long project, nor should it result in a 300-page document. I have created policies multiple times. The key is getting the right stakeholders in the room, agreeing on what is most important, and understanding that you are creating a set of *guidelines*, not a book! The goal is not to create a policy manual no one will read; instead, the goal is to create a policy that is one or two pages that can be posted where everyone can see it. In fact, the policy should be posted at everyone's desk.

## Ask the Right Questions

Questions you should ask are as follows:

1. **Who needs the policy?** (Ideally, this should apply to every employee, volunteer, board member, vendor, agency, and so on.) Anyone who might submit social media content on behalf of your organization or business needs to know about the policy and receive training.

2. **Who will write the policy?** Ideally it should be written by a marketing person, not an attorney. You can simply use the templates available at http://socialmedia.org/disclosure/.

3. **Who will train your staff?** Training is an important part of creating a social media ethics policy and it is part of the Federal Trade Commission mandate. Again, in an ideal situation, this would be conducted by a marketing person, not an attorney. Additional questions for you:

4. How will HR train new employees, volunteers, and others in your social media policy?

5. Who will train new board members, vendors, and others in your social media policy?

6. Who can be the social media "ambassador" to answer questions?

## Changing Labor Issues

One area for all businesses and organizations to understand is that the National Labor Relations Board (NLRB) protects certain employee statements about the workplace on social media. Rulings have been changing over the last few years and continue to evolve, so it is important to stay up to date with these changes. One of the best sources I have found is www.jdsupra.com. Here you can sign up for e-mail updates and alerts on social media and NLRB rulings. The site offers updates from attorneys and law firms around the country on ethics, social media, NLRB, and many other issues. Because of the changing nature of the rulings, it is difficult to cite some here, but generally speaking, here is what the NLRB has tended to rule in favor of:

The NLRB has tended to protect employee comments about the workplace on social media sites. Attorney Patrick Pearce, of Ogden Murphy Wallace, PLLC, practices with the firm's Employment and Labor and Hospitality groups. Pearce writes as follows:

"On August 22, 2014, the National Labor Relations Board (NLRB) ruled against a non-union restaurant based on management terminating employees as the result of the employees' Facebook postings. Unhappy employees posted comments to Facebook regarding the situation, and the employer responded by terminating employees who had posted. The

Board ordered that the employees be reinstated and receive back pay, lost benefits, and removal of the discharge records from the employee personnel files. The decision illustrates why both unionized and non-union employers need to be aware of the Board's positions on employee use of social media. The basis for the NLRB aggressively pursuing the issue is the Board's position that social media postings may constitute "concerted activity" protected by the National Labor Relations Act (NLRA). The NLRA may apply regardless of whether the employer is union or non-union, and the Board enforces the Act based on its interpretations of the Act's provisions." (sipandnosh.com 2014)

Pearce goes on with the caution: There are several considerations for management following this decision:

"Be aware that regardless of union presence, the Board may have jurisdiction over an employer. The Board has been more aggressive in recent years in pursuing potential violations of the NLRA against non-union employers. Employers need to know that simply lacking a union presence will not protect them against Board enforcement action if they are not acting in compliance with the NLRA." (sipandnosh.com 2014)

Be cautious when considering disciplining employees based on social media use. Under the NLRA, employees are entitled to discuss terms and conditions of employment with other workers. Employers need to be careful before taking action. For example, a negative posting on hours or wages by one employee that is responded to by other employees may be protected as multiple workers are discussing protected issues, making the discussions potentially protected "concerted activity." A negative posting by one worker that does not generate any responses or discussion may instead be considered "griping" and not protected under the NLRA. Each situation will have to be assessed on its particular facts. (sipandnosh.com 2014)

Check and possibly rewrite organization social media and communication policies. The Board has been increasingly aggressive over the last several years in scrutinizing both union and nonunion employer social media and communication policies and practices. Many organizations have policies written before the Board began pursuing the social media issue. These policies may not be in compliance with current Board interpretations of the NLRA and what employees are allowed to post or discuss online. Employers should double-check to make sure that practices and policies are consistent with what is permissible under the Act as the Board interprets it. (sipandnosh.com 2014)

## Summary

In this chapter, we have discussed the issue of what to consider when creating a social media ethics policy. You need to be aware of what you can and can't mandate based on law.

There are excellent social media ethics policy templates available at http://socialmedia.org/disclosure/

# CHAPTER 8

# Steps to Create a Social Media Ethics Policy

## Every Business Should Have a Social Media Policy

This is not my advice; it comes from the Federal Trade Commission (FTC). It is also a smart business practice.

One aspect of the FTC guidelines explains why every business, for-profit, nonprofit, educational, faith based, and others, should have a social media policy. ***"This is to protect the business and to help insure there is proper disclosure for consumers."***

The guidelines make it very clear:

1. You will require disclosure and truthfulness in social media posts about your business by *anyone* connected to your business.
2. You will create a social media policy and train employees and stakeholders.
3. You will monitor social media conversations about your business and correct mistakes when proper disclosure does not happen.

If your business does not take these steps, your business can be 100-percent liable for missteps.

This means that businesses should:

1. Create the policy.
2. Train current employees, board members, vendors, marketing partners, volunteers, and others so they understand the social media policy.
3. Train new employees, board members, vendors, marketing partners, volunteers, and others so they understand the social media policy.
4. Have appropriate people in leadership accountable for making sure the policy is followed.

So perhaps by now you are asking what is the difference between a *"guide"* and the *"law? "* Here is what the FTC says:

"Guides are administrative interpretations of laws administered by the Commission. Although guides do not have the force and effect of law, if a person or company fails to comply with a guide, the Commission might bring an enforcement action alleging an unfair or deceptive practice in violation of the FTC Act." (DiResta 2013)

## Bottom Line: Create a Social Media Ethics Policy and Train Your Staff or You Place Your Business or Organization at Risk

Using social media and asking employees to participate can be a powerful marketing tool. Executives like Tony Hsieh, founder and CEO of Zappos, require their new employees to take social networking classes during onboarding. Dell has even developed a brand community to foster employee and customer advocacy on social media (Pollitt 2013).

How should you proceed?

Step one: Define your goals.

Step two: Know which platforms you want to use and why. (This should be based on research knowing where your current and potential customers have conversations.)

Step three: Get into action now!

***Think of a social media policy as a code of conduct.*** It helps employees and stakeholders know the do's and don'ts of posting. One expert explains the reasoning for a social media policy this way: "A social media policy defines your team's roles, rules and responsibilities and establishes guidelines to communicate consistently. It also lets your team know how to prevent or respond to a crisis." (Demetrio 2013)

A social media guide can benefit your organization in many ways, but most importantly, it can contribute to

1. Providing structure for employees
2. Protecting your brand and business
3. Educating and guiding employees to being "ambassadors"

4. Creating value for the organization as employees know the right way to act, which reflects positively on the brand

5. Showing you are a modern and transparent company (mindjumpers. com 2013)

## Less Is More: Creating a Social Media Policy Should Not Become an Exercise in Complexity

I was once sitting at a meeting in Seattle of corporate compliance officers and human resource executives from some of the nation's biggest businesses. In chatting with a compliance officer sitting next to me (for a global company), I asked her about their social media policy.

She told me it was in process and up to 300 pages. I was aghast! "Three hundred pages" I said. *"No one will read or remember 300 pages!"*

I went on to help her understand that whether an employee is 18 years old or 40 years old, a social media policy should be straightforward, simple, and easily remembered; and that you cannot anticipate every possibility.

That is what this chapter is about, helping you understand how to create a social media policy that will help conform to the FTC guidelines, give your employees and stakeholders guidance, and help protect your reputation, whether you are an individual, for-profit, nonprofit, educational, or faith-based organization.

An excellent source for creating a social media policy can be found at this website: socialmedia.org/disclosure. It is licensed under a Creative Commons Attribution 3.0 Unported License. Attribute it to SocialMedia.org and link to www.socialmedia.org/disclosure." (SocialMedia.org 2014)

Here you will find several pages (in Microsoft Word or Adobe PDF format) of boilerplate that allow virtually any business or organization to cut, paste, and create a social media policy. You will find templates for employees, board members, vendors, bloggers, and many more. Use these; they are invaluable. Credit should be given to Andy Sernovitz, the author of the book *Word of Mouth Marketing* and the person behind SocialMedia.org.

As outlined by Andy and his team, you will find the scenarios addressed in these templates include the following:

- Disclosure of Identity
- Personal and Unofficial Social Media Participation
- Social Media Outreach Campaigns
- Truthfulness
- Advocacy Programs
- Compensation and Incentives
- Agency and Contractor Disclosure
- Vendor Questionnaire
- Monitor and Respond
- Policies and Training
- Creative Flexibility
- General Best Practices

## Key: The Policy Is Constantly Evolving

It is important to understand that when you create a social media policy, it should be a living, evolving document.

Why is it so important to create the policy for your organization? Enlisting the help of employees and stakeholders to share stories of your brand is a powerful marketing tool, if used correctly. In addition, the FTC has made it clear that the best way to protect your company from legal trouble is by establishing formal disclosure policies for your staff, agencies, and subcontractors (SocialMedia.org 2014).

How complicated is it to use these templates to create a social media policy? It should not be that complicated or that time-consuming. I have used the templates and they are very simple to tailor for any business or organization.

While Chief Marketing Officer for a major nonprofit organization in Seattle with 26,000 members and thousands more as volunteers, I used these templates to create a social media policy that would address employees, members, volunteers, board members, and vendors. By using the templates, I created the policy in two weeks and then did training sessions for employees and volunteers.

Who should be trained? Employees, volunteers, board members, vendors, marketing partners, and yes interns.

Start early. At Unisys, new hires are briefed on social media policies practically before the ink on their contracts is even dry. It is literally one of the steps necessary to activate new hires' employment (Meister 2012).

At Sprint, the social media-training brand is called Sprint Ninja. Sprint employees who complete the Sprint Social Media Ninjas program complete a two-hour workshop to receive their Ninja certificate (Meister 2012).

When training, use clear examples to help stakeholders understand what you are describing. Examples of proper and improper Facebook posts, tweets, blog posts, and so on, will help team members understand exactly what your expectations are.

Ask questions, engage, and make sure people in training sessions understand. This is not about distributing a policy memo, it is about helping stakeholders and employees understand what is proper and improper. Use simple terms and help people understand why there is a policy and what is at stake.

According to Eric Tung writing in SocialMediaExaminer.com (Tung 2014), "Social media policies must meet company and legal requirements, but should include open opportunities for employees to support your social media efforts." (Tung 2014)

He goes on to say, "Research shows that a majority of employees are willing to share company information—they're just not sure what to share because they don't want to get in trouble." (Tung 2014)

Among the nine components of a good policy, Tung advocates some important points:

- Does the company want multiple policies to address various departments and networks; one combined detailed policy; or one general policy to apply to the company as a whole?
- Navigating how state and federal laws affect your company's social media policy takes time, but it is imperative. You do not want to be fined for not abiding by the law. Research

the NLRB and other federal labor laws that may protect
social media posts. Some states have enacted laws that
prohibit employers from requesting usernames or passwords.
(Tung 2014)

Here are some questions you may have about policies and practices:

1. Can I use a #hashtag as disclosure?
   a. The FTC has not specifically said hashtag use would or would
      not make a disclosure compliant; however, as we have covered in
      Chapter 3, there have been cases in which the FTC fined busi-
      nesses citing the fact that specific #hashtags did not constitute
      disclosure.
2. Can I say the word "Ad" at the start of a post and comply with disclosure rules?
   a. The FTC has stated that disclosure must be *clear and conspicu-
      ous* so consumers clearly understand what they are reading. The
      key in this example is whether the consumer clearly understands
      he or she is being "sold to" before reading or taking action to
      purchase. (Tung 2014)

**Key Point:** FTC regulations have traditionally been associated with
advertising. However, the federal government makes no distinction between PR and advertising. In this age of strategic communication, PR
practitioners have to be aware of all social media regulations. Given that
social media management is increasingly under the purview of public relations, knowing these regulatory boundaries are important for all PR
firms, departments, and practitioners.

The Word of Mouth Marketing Association (WOMMA) has been
among those working to clarify the FTC's disclosure guidelines.

In 2013, attorney Anthony DiResta posted a lengthy article on the
WOMMA website, explaining the Dot Com Disclosure guidelines.

In DiResta's comments, he stated as follows:

"Twitter: The bottom line for the FTC is that consumers need to
understand the indicator, be it #ad or something else, and be aware that it
means that the message is a sponsored endorsement. An advertiser is only

responsible for the message that it sends or that are sent by its agents." (DiResta 2013)

"Instagram: If a picture such as one posted to Instagram or Pinterest makes a claim about a product, it may require a disclosure. The key is how the consumer will understand the picture. If consumers would understand a picture to be an endorsement of a commercial product by, say, a celebrity who uses Instagram, then a disclosure would be necessary." (DiResta 2013)

"Hyperlinks: The issue of when hyperlinks can be effective in meeting FTC disclosure requirements is an important one. In evaluating the effectiveness of hyperlink disclosures, the language of the label of the hyperlink is critical. When a consumer clicks on a link, he or she should be taken directly to the necessary disclosure information. The consumer should not have to click a hyperlink and then navigate to another page or search through distracting information on the page to read the disclosure." (DiResta 2013)

## What Does a Sample Policy Look Like?

SocialMedia.org's Three Guides for Safe Social Media Outreach summarizes the fundamental obligations required for marketers to stay safe:

1. Require disclosure and truthfulness in social media outreach.
2. Monitor the conversation and correct misstatements.
3. Create social media policies and training programs.

The FTC has also made it clear that the best way to protect your company from legal trouble is by establishing formal disclosure policies for your staff, agencies, and subcontractors." www.socialmedia.org/disclosure

## Summary

In this chapter, I have explained how to write a social media ethics policy and strongly suggested you use the templates provided at www.socialmedia.org/disclosure.

## SocialMedia.org's Disclosure Best Practices Checklist 1: Disclosure of Identity

The following is from SocialMedia.org's disclosure toolkit. This is just one of several toolkit pages available for your use under Issued under Creative Commons Attribution 3.0 Unported License (www.socialmedia. org/disclosure)

### Focus: Best practices for how employees and agencies acting as official corporate representatives disclose their identity when using social media.

When communicating via social media on behalf of our company or on topics related to the business of our company, we will

1. Disclose who we are, who we work for, and any other relevant affiliations from the very first encounter.
2. Disclose any business/client relationship if we are communicating on behalf of another party.
3. Ensure that all disclosure meets the minimum legal standard by being (a) clear and conspicuous, (b) understandable by the average reader, and (c) clearly visible within the relevant content.
4. Require all employees to disclose their employer when using social media to communicate on behalf of the company or about company-related topics.
5. Make certain that disclosure is sufficient so that the average reader understands that our company is responsible for the content, while they are reading the content.
6. Comply with all laws and regulations regarding disclosure of identity.
7. Properly use pseudonyms and role accounts:
   - (Option A) Never use a false or obscured identity or pseudonym.
   - (Option B) If aliases or role accounts are used for employee privacy, security, or other business reasons, these identities will clearly indicate the organization represented and provide means for two-way communications with that alias.

8. Provide a means of communicating with our company in order to verify our involvement in a particular item of social media content.

9. Instruct all employees, agencies, and advocates with whom we have a formal relationship on these disclosure policies and require them to comply.

The following is from SocialMedia.org's disclosure toolkit. This is just one of several toolkit pages available for your use under Issued under Creative Commons Attribution 3.0 Unported License. (www.socialmedia.org/disclosure)

### Focus: Best practices for employees who talk about company-related issues at any time in their personal social media participation.

For personal social media interactions:

1. If employees write anything related to the business of their employer on personal pages, posts, and comments, they will clearly identify their business affiliation.

2. The manner of disclosure can be flexible as long as it is (a) clear and conspicuous, (b) understandable by the average reader, and (c) clearly visible within the relevant content. (e.g., disclosure methods could include usernames that include the company name, or a statement in the post or comment itself, "I work for __<company>__ and this is my personal opinion.")

3. Employees will specifically clarify which post or comments are their own opinions vs. official corporate statements.

4. Writing that does not mention work-related topics does not need to mention the employment relationship.

5. If employees post or comment anonymously, they should not discuss matters related to the business of their employer. If employer-related topics are mentioned, they should disclose their affiliation with the company.

# CHAPTER 9

# The Legal Backlash

## Businesses Suing Consumers After They Post Negative Social Media Posts About Their Consumer Experience

A developing legal and ethical issue in emerging media is whether a business has the right to sue and win in court against a consumer who received what they believe was poor service or a bad product and posted a negative review.

Simply do a Google search with this or a similar phrase and many stories immediately pop up: "businesses sue over negative social media posts."

One consumer who was angry over what she thought was poor work on her home logged onto Yelp and posted negative reviews about the firm that did the work, including claims that some of her jewelry was missing. The contractor filed a $750,000 Internet defamation lawsuit against the consumer saying the postings on Yelp and Angie's List were false the court for a preliminary injunction to keep her from writing similar reviews. (Mataconis 2014)

Lawyers say it is one of a growing number of defamation lawsuits over online reviews on sites such as Yelp, Angie's List, and TripAdvisor and over Internet postings in general. They say the freewheeling and acerbic world of web speech is colliding with the ever-growing importance of online reputations for businesses, doctors, restaurants, and even teachers. No one keeps track of how many suits are filed over online reviews, and lawyers say the numbers are still small but are getting larger. (outsidethebeltway.com 2014)

In another case, Hotel Quebec sued a former guest for $95,000. The reason? The guest wrote a negative review on TripAdvisor, exposing the bed bugs in his room and refused to remove the review.

This is clearly an interesting case, and it triggers a number of questions:

- Under what circumstances can a hotel ask guests to remove reviews from sites such as TripAdvisor?
- When a customer has evidence (videotape, pictures) to prove his or her review, can a business still go ahead and sue the customer because of potential loss in business?
- Will such a case set a precedent that will have guests think twice before writing negative reviews?

In yet another case, a Southwest Airlines worker sued a passenger over tweets blasting customer service. According to BusinessInsider. com, a singer from Nashville was sued by a Southwest Airlines employee for firing off a series of tweets, blasting the company's customer service. The singer had taken to Twitter to vent her frustrations after a Southwest employee barred her from boarding a plane early with her children, according to the lawsuit (via Consumerist). The passenger had purchased Business Select tickets for herself and one child, but not for her other children and her husband, who were traveling with her. When she tried to board early with her entire family, she was told that only those passengers with Business Select tickets could come along, according to Patterson's lawsuit. The passenger, upset that her 4-year-old child could not board the plane early with her, vented to her 187,000 Twitter followers, mentioning the gate agent's name. The gate agent sued the passenger for defamation, saying it put her in a false light. (BusinessInsider.com 2014)

Lawyers say such cases are a cautionary tale for a new era: Those who feel targeted by defamation on the Web are more likely to file suit, and judges and juries are more likely to take such claims seriously than in years past, raising the legal stakes over vitriolic reviews, nasty blog comments, and Facebook feuds. (outsidethebeltway.com 2014)

Part of this emerging issue comes down to communications—could the problems have been solved before the issue went public?

Second: If someone posts a negative review, are they posting an opinion or statements of fact? There is a difference.

The following is from attorney's who are experts in this field posting on JDSupra.com:

Before you vent online, sort out your facts and opinions (and understand what each will mean in a defamation claim).

Attorney Travis Crabtree of Gray Reed & McGraw explains, "Opinions cannot be the basis of a defamation claim, but facts can. That distinction can be a difficult one to make when in the middle of an online rant, so the main point is that reviewers should be able to back-up any factual claim, or claim that can be considered factual. Calling a dry cleaner lousy won't get you in trouble. Saying they refused to return your shirt because they were wearing it can land you in court. Calling them thieves gets a little trickier." (JDSupra.com 2014)

Jamie Nafziger, a partner at law firm Dorsey & Whitney, echoes the view thusly: "The most important things users can do to protect themselves from liability for negative reviews are to (1) be sure their posts contain honest opinions and (2) be sure that to the extent posts contain facts, the facts are truthful. If users are including facts, they should link to their sources, if possible. Lying or exaggerating can land a user in court. Posting flaming remarks, abusive comments, or lies also may tarnish the user's reputation or result in the user being banned from participating in a social network. Don't stop posting reviews—just be sure your reviews are truthful and based on your personal experience!" (JDSupra.com 2014)

For businesses, comes this advice:

*"Consider bad reviews as valuable, constructive feedback:* Attorney Jeff Van Hoosear at Knobbe offers an additional, very worthwhile perspective on an alternative to legal action: "Online negative reviews should still be treated as 'customer feedback' and used constructively by the business. Is there a problem that needs to be addressed? If so, address it, and let the reviewers know you've addressed it. Even if a business feels the reviews are unfair or untruthful—it should still reach out to the reviewers with an apology and offer to make it right.

Lawyering up should be reserved for the egregious case that goes beyond the negative and attacks the integrity of a business's products or services. (JDSupra.com 2014)

Here is the most important factor in all of this: Some businesses are said to be adding in phrases to their terms and conditions, which many people do not read, that could penalize consumers for posting negative reviews.

The following analysis is from (blankrome.com 2014). Many dentists, wedding photographers, moving companies, locksmiths, and online retailers have each tried to limit negative online customer reviews via non-disparagement clauses in their service agreements.

Traditionally found in negotiated settlement or employee severance agreements, non-disparagement (or "no review") clauses are now making their way into non-negotiated service contracts and the oft-ignored terms and conditions of online retailers. So the question becomes: Are non-disparagement clauses the wave of the future, or simply the next battleground in the war for online consumer rights?

In its simplest form, a non-disparagement clause seeks to prevent a customer or receiver of goods or services from posting negative reviews about a service provider or vendor by outlining the financial repercussions for any violation.

The impetus behind companies inserting these clauses is the popularity of review sites like Yelp.com, RipoffReport.com, Dine.com, TripAdvisor.com, and Amazon.com—coupled with the increasing number of people turning to such sites in choosing which companies to do business with. Because a poor review can be financially devastating, businesses want to prevent clients from bad-mouthing them—even if the criticism is true.

Still, the first issue regarding any non-negotiable, non-disparagement clause is whether it is enforceable. According to University of California, Los Angeles constitutional law professor Eugene Volokh in a Wall Street Journal article titled, "You Ruined My Wedding—And You're Suing Me?" the answer, not surprisingly, is: It depends.

As a general rule, items agreed to in a contract are enforceable. But the "gotcha factor" is critical, Volokh told *The Wall Street Journal*. If a reasonable consumer would be very surprised by a clause in a vendor contract or a terms of service agreement, that provision may be deemed unenforceable. "You could see some of these [non-disparagement clauses] invalidated," Volokh said. "This will be decided on a state-by-state level."

Consumers should be careful when reading a non-negotiable service agreement, so as to be aware of any nondisparagement or similar clauses. This is especially true when dealing with an online retailer's terms of service—which may be separate from the specific contractual provisions.

Businesses can also take steps to ensure their reputations are protected without impugning free speech. According to one commentator, a more defensible approach is to require a consumer to take their complaint to the company before posting anything online; in exchange, the consumer receives a coupon (or other item of value). This approach would not ban comments indefinitely.

But even setting aside the legal issues, public perception of companies using nondisparagement clauses may also be worth considering. Such clauses may send the message that a company does not stand behind its work, or is overly concerned with bad press. While a few negative reviews may be the cost of doing business, the overall impact will be negated by more positive reviews.

As businesses continue to take concerted steps to protect their online reputations, and consumers continue to post online, this area of law is likely to develop. The introduction of pro-consumer legislation will only quicken the pace. But until then, the battle for online consumer rights carries on. (blankrome.com 2014)

## Summary

In this chapter, I have discussed the backlash by some businesses over what they consider to be unfair reviews from customers, and how some businesses are now "tucking in" non-disparagement clauses in their "terms and conditions."

# CHAPTER 10

# Emerging/Future Issues

## The Big Emerging Issues

There are many issues affecting marketing and consumers in the field of emerging media; some of the most important are given below:

- Consumer privacy
- Mobile tracking of consumer locations
- Marketers collecting and selling consumer data that end up in the hands of data brokers
- Social media disclosure by businesses
- Businesses suing consumers after they post negative social media posts about their consumer experience

## Consumer Privacy

This is a topic that is changing so rapidly we almost need to check Google News daily to stay up to date with the latest developments.

As *The Wall Street Journal* (WSJ) reports, "Companies today are increasingly tying people's real-life identities to their online browsing habits." (Valentino-Devries and Singer-Vine 2012)

The question is whether this is good for marketers and consumers, or only beneficial to marketers.

The WSJ reports, "The use of real identities across the Web is going mainstream at a rapid clip." A Wall Street Journal examination of nearly 1,000 top websites found that 75 percent now include code from social networks, such as Facebook's "Like" or Twitter's "Tweet" buttons. Such code can match people's identities with their web-browsing activities on an unprecedented scale and can even track a user's arrival on a page if the button is never clicked (Angwin and Valentino-Devries 2012).

In separate research, the Journal examined what happens when people logged in to roughly 70 popular websites that request a login and found that more than a quarter of the time, the sites passed along a user's real name, e-mail address or other personal details, such as username, to third-party companies. One major dating site passed along a person's self-reported sexual orientation and drug-use habits to advertising companies (Angwin and Valentino-Devries 2012).

An excellent source of stories about consumer privacy can be found at http://online.wsj.com/public/page/what-they-know-digital-privacy.html

Two browser add-ons that can help reduce tracking when you browse the web are: Ghostery and Disconnect.

## Mobile Tracking of Consumer Locations

Cell phone tracking is now pitting consumers against retailers in many ways, and once again, privacy is at the heart of the issue.

According to the FTC, about a thousand new mobile applications (apps) enter the market each day. They raise significant privacy issues and carry equally significant liability issues for those who develop or sponsor them (i.e., the company that creates them), and even for those who simply market them. In February 2013, the FTC released a report, Mobile Privacy Disclosures: Building Trust Through Transparency, that outlined numerous best practices concerning the making, marketing, and use of mobile applications (Greenberg and Kates 2013).

According to author Chuck Martin, *Mobile Influence: The New Power of the Consumer* (2013), "Product tracking has gotten very sophisticated over time, with RFID (radio frequency identification) chips and readers and other inventory-tracking systems. Combined with mobile tracking technologies, the logical next step is to link the product locations and products with mobile shoppers and their behaviors and current needs. The goal would be to make the trips through the aisles faster and the exit from the transaction points more efficient and friction-free for the consumer." This can be good for marketers, but is this what consumers want? Should consumers have the option to opt in for tracking?

New technologies now allow retailers to use cell phone signals to track shoppers as they move around the store—including the aisles where they spend the most time, if they make a purchase, and how often they return to the store. Some technologies, such as iBeacon, require that customers download a mobile app, turn on Bluetooth, accept location services, and opt in so they can be tracked and receive in-store notifications (Levitt 2014).

Other approaches, pioneered by analytics startups such as Nomi and Euclid, use sensors to pick up signals emitted from any Wi-Fi-enabled cell phone. This means that any consumer who walks into a store (or even walks by a store) with his or her cell phone turned on may be automatically tracked—without knowledge or explicit consent. (Nomi and Euclid both say that they collect nonidentifiable data and offer opt-out agreements). (Levitt 2014)

Industry research shows that consumers overwhelmingly reject cell phone tracking. In a recent OpinionLab study of 1,042 consumers, 77 percent said that in-store cell phone tracking was unacceptable, and 81 percent said that they didn't trust retailers to keep their data private and secure. The biggest concerns are that retailers will not keep the data safe (68.5 percent); tracking feels like spying (67 percent); and retailers will use the data exclusively to their own benefit (60.5 percent) (Levitt 2014).

Opt-in seems to be the heart of the issue. When asked about the best way for retailers to approach in-store tracking, 64 percent of consumers said that the best approach is opt-in, versus a mere 12 percent who stated that shoppers should be automatically tracked (Levitt 2014).

## Marketers Collecting and Selling Consumer Data to Data Brokers

In 2014, CBS News and 60 Minutes broadcast a groundbreaking story called "The Data Brokers: Selling your personal information." (CBSNews .com 2014)

Companies and marketing firms have been gathering information about customers and potential customers for years, collecting their names and addresses, tracking credit card purchases, and asking them to fill out questionnaires, so they can offer discounts and send catalogues. But today, we are giving up more and more private information online without knowing that it is being harvested and personalized and sold to lots of different people...our likes and dislikes, our closest friends, our bad habits, even your daily movements, both on and offline. Federal Trade Commissioner Julie Brill says we have lost control of our most personal information. (CBSNews.com 2014)

No one even knows how many companies there are trafficking in our data. But it is certainly in the thousands, and would include research firms, all sorts of Internet companies, advertisers, retailers, and trade associations. The largest data broker is Acxiom, a marketing giant that brags it has, on average, 1,500 pieces of information on more than 200 million Americans. (CBSNews.com 2014)

Every piece of data about us now seems to be worth something to somebody. And lots more people are giving up information about people they do business with, from state Departments of Motor Vehicles, to pizza parlors. (CBSNews.com 2014)

Tim Sparapani says it is a lot. He has been following the data broker industry for years, first as a privacy lawyer for the American Civil Liberties Union, then as Facebook's first director of public policy. He is currently advising tech companies and app makers. Sparapani thinks people would be stunned to learn what is being compiled about them and sold, and might end up in their profiles: religion, ethnicity, political affiliations, user names, income, and family medical history. And that is just for openers. Tim Sparapani: Most retailers are finding out that they have a secondary source of income, which is that the data about their customers is probably just about as valuable, maybe even more so, than the actual product or service that they are selling to the individual. So, there is a whole new revenue stream that many companies have found. (CBSNews. com 2014)

## Summary

In this chapter, I have discussed some of the most important emerging issues, including consumer privacy, mobile tracking of consumer locations, businesses selling consumer data to data brokers, and businesses suing consumers after they post negative social media posts about their consumer experience.

# CHAPTER 11

# What You Can Do to Make a Difference?

## Pause Before You Post!

This sounds simplistic, but it is the best piece of advice I can give: *Pause before you post.*

Every post demonstrates you as a brand, your professionalism, your values, and your ethics.

If someone shows pictures boozing at a party, that is their brand. If you work for a business or organization and you do undercover posts on behalf of the business without disclosing your relationship with the business, you have demonstrated your ethics. If you are unhappy about a product or service and post a rant that goes far beyond the facts, you are misusing the gift of social media platforms.

We are in an era when we can share, review, ask questions about products and services like never before. These are gifts that should be treated with care. If we misuse these gifts like posting fake reviews, people will stop having faith in consumer product reviews.

Setting the stage for appropriate business behavior is important in every business. We establish our mission, values, and frequently the ethics we stand for. Unfortunately, in most businesses, we forget one of the most important aspects of business: social media.

These are the platforms where our potential and current customers have conversations. These are the platforms we should be listening to. This is an area that should have an ethics policy so everyone connected to a business or organization knows the dos and don'ts, and why.

These concepts should be outlined in high schools, higher education, business and organizations, faith-based organizations, and nonprofits.

Create the policy, train people, have discussions about social media ethics on an on-going basis, learn, share, and teach.

It is important to remind everyone that *everything we do on the Internet is public.* There is no expectation of privacy; those days are gone. Who you follow, who you friend, what you post, is public and will be available forever. We need to conduct ourselves with transparency and complete professionalism. We must remember we are all legally responsible for what we post.

It is ironic to think that many years ago the great CBS journalist Edward R. Murrow shared a famous quote about television. In some ways, that same quote can be applied to computers:

*"This instrument can teach, it can illuminate; yes, and it can even inspire. But it can do so only to the extent that humans are determined to use it to those ends. Otherwise it is merely wires and lights in a box." (Murrow 1958)*

This topic will only achieve the goals we want if you take this book and become a true advocate for creating a world of higher standards. It is up to you.

## What Can You Do Ahead of Time?

Plenty. If you are interviewing for a job, ask what their social media policy is. Find out how knowledgeable they are about *disclosure*, if they have a policy and training plan in place. If they do not, share what you have learned and help them understand what is at stake and why they need a policy.

## What Should You Do When Confronted with the Issues?

There have been many cases in which employees or friends have been "asked" or "strongly encouraged" to post fake reviews about products or services. It may come from a boss, coworker, business associate, or friend. If someone asks you to do this, you now know it is illegal; it is problematic for the business, the person asking you to do this, and problematic for you.

What can you do? Help the person asking you to post a fake review to understand what is at stake:

Their reputation
Your reputation
The reputation of the business
A possible FTC fine
Negative news coverage

Remember, *you always have choice.* The choice you make will determine what you believe is the difference between right and wrong.

# CHAPTER 12

# Sample Social Media Ethics Policies

The following is an excerpt taken from the Federal Trade Commission document on Disclosure, .comDisclosure (FTC 2013) in Brief, available at www.ftc.gov/sites/default/files/attachments/press-releases/ftc-staff-revises-online-advertising-disclosure-guidelines/130312dotcomdisclosures.pdf

## Overview

In the online marketplace, consumers can transact business without the constraints of time or distance. One can log on to the Internet day or night and purchase almost anything one desires, and advances in mobile technology allow advertisers to reach consumers nearly anywhere they go. But cyberspace is not without boundaries, and deception is unlawful no matter what the medium. The FTC has enforced and will continue enforcing its consumer protection laws to ensure that products and services are described truthfully online, and that consumers understand what they are paying for. These activities benefit consumers as well as sellers, who expect and deserve the opportunity to compete in a marketplace free of deception and unfair practices.

The general principles of advertising law apply online, but new issues arise almost as fast as technology develops—most recently, new issues have arisen concerning space-constrained screens and social media platforms. This FTC staff guidance document describes the information businesses should consider as they develop ads for online media to ensure that they comply with the law.

Briefly,

1. The same consumer protection laws that apply to commercial activities in other media apply online, including activities in the mobile

marketplace. The FTC Act's prohibition on "unfair or deceptive acts or practices" encompasses online advertising, marketing, and sales. In addition, many Commission rules and guides are not limited to any particular medium used to disseminate claims or advertising, and therefore, apply to the wide spectrum of online activities.

2. When practical, advertisers should incorporate relevant limitations and qualifying information into the underlying claim, rather than having a separate disclosure qualifying the claim.

3. Required disclosures must be clear and conspicuous. In evaluating whether a disclosure is likely to be clear and conspicuous, advertisers should consider its placement in the ad and its proximity to the relevant claim. The closer the disclosure is to the claim to which it relates, the better. Additional considerations include: the prominence of the disclosure; whether it is unavoidable; whether other parts of the ad distract attention from the disclosure; whether the disclosure needs to be repeated at different places on a website; whether disclosures in audio messages are presented in an adequate volume and cadence; whether visual disclosures appear for a sufficient duration; and whether the language of the disclosure is understandable to the intended audience.

4. To make a disclosure clear and conspicuous, advertisers should: Place the disclosure as close as possible to the triggering claim.

Take account of the various devices and platforms consumers may use to view advertising and any corresponding disclosure. If an ad is viewable on a particular device or platform, any necessary disclosures should be sufficient to prevent the ad from being misleading when viewed on that device or platform.

When a space-constrained ad requires a disclosure, incorporate the disclosure into the ad whenever possible. However, when it is not possible to make a disclosure in a space-constrained ad, it may, under some circumstances, be acceptable to make the disclosure clearly and conspicuously on the page to which the ad links.

When using a hyperlink to lead to a disclosure, make the link obvious; label the hyperlink appropriately to convey the importance, nature, and relevance of the information it leads to; use hyperlink styles consistently so that consumers know when a link is available; place the hyperlink as close as possible to the relevant information it qualifies and make it noticeable; take consumers directly to the disclosure on the click-through page; assess the effectiveness of the hyperlink by monitoring click-through rates and other information about consumer use and make changes accordingly.

Preferably, design advertisements so that "scrolling" is not necessary in order to find a disclosure. When scrolling is necessary, use text or visual cues to encourage consumers to scroll to view the disclosure.

Keep abreast of empirical research about where consumers do and do not look on a screen.

Recognize and respond to any technological limitations or unique characteristics of a communication method when making disclosures.

Display disclosures before consumers make a decision to buy—for example, before they "add to shopping cart." Also recognize that disclosures may have to be repeated before purchase to ensure that they are adequately presented to consumers.

- Repeat disclosures, as needed, on lengthy websites and in connection with repeated claims. Disclosures may also have to be repeated if consumers have multiple routes through a website.
- If a product or service promoted online is intended to be (or can be) purchased from "brick and mortar" stores or from online retailers other than the advertiser itself, then any disclosure necessary to prevent deception or unfair injury should be presented in the ad itself—that is, before consumers head to a store or some other online retailer.
- Necessary disclosures should not be relegated to "terms of use" and similar contractual agreements.
- Prominently display disclosures so they are noticeable to consumers, and evaluate the size, color, and graphic treatment of the disclosure in relation to other parts of the webpage.
- Review the entire ad to assess whether the disclosure is effective in light of other elements—text, graphics, hyperlinks, or sound—that might distract consumers' attention from the disclosure.

- Use audio disclosures when making audio claims, and present them in a volume and cadence so that consumers can hear and understand them.
- Display visual disclosures for a duration sufficient for consumers to notice, read, and understand them.
- Use plain language and syntax so that consumers understand the disclosures.

5. If a disclosure is necessary to prevent an advertisement from being deceptive, unfair, or otherwise violative of a Commission rule, and it is not possible to make the disclosure clearly and conspicuously, then that ad should not be disseminated. This means that if a particular platform does not provide an opportunity to make clear and conspicuous disclosures, then that platform should not be used to disseminate advertisements that require disclosures.

Negative consumer experiences can result in lost consumer goodwill and erode consumer confidence. Clear, conspicuous, and meaningful disclosures benefit advertisers and consumers.

## Sample Social Media Policies

We can learn much from some of the best ethics and social media policies. As examples, we recommend you review some of these to better understand the best practices.

## Mayo Clinic Social Media Policy

http://sharing.mayoclinic.org/guidelines/for-mayo-clinic-employees/
The Mayo Clinic policy is an excellent example because it is easy to understand and includes practical advice. It also ties social media to Mayo Clinic policies and confidential information. In addition, the Mayo Clinic policy addresses guidance on "friending."

## Coca-Cola Social Media Policy

www.coca-colacompany.com/stories/online-social-media-principles

The Coca-Cola social media policy is an excellent example because the policy includes some important language about what the company stands for, and the vision of its brands. It is written in easy-to-understand language, includes company commitments and what social media participants should commit to.

Coca-Cola's policy also includes a section addressing the ". . .use excessive tracking software, adware, malware or spyware."

## Dell Social Media Policy

www.dell.com/learn/us/en/uscorp1/corp-comm/social-media-policy?
c=us&l=en&s=corp

Dell has a very interesting social media policy because ". . ..it encourages all employees to use Social Media the right way." How committed is Dell? The company has "Social Media and Communities University (SMaC U) classes."

Dell stresses disclosure and transparency in their policy and offers stakeholders appropriate guidance on how to best engage in social media marketing. The company also includes a nice quote that sets the atmosphere: "Be Nice, Have Fun and Connect."

## Gartner Public Web Participation Guidelines

http://blogs.gartner.com/gartner-public-web-participation-guidelines/

We would expect a company like Gartner to not only inform, but also educate us about the issues. Gartner goes beyond social media and offers "Web Participation" guidelines, which includes ". . .blogs, microblogs, linkblogs, social network sites, wikis, bookmark sites, content sharing sites (e.g., photo, video, image or document), forums, mailing lists, discussion groups and chat rooms."

The company makes it quite clear that the guidelines apply to ". . .all Gartner associates, wherever located, including analysts who participate in the Gartner Blogger Network."

A simple-but-powerful part of the policy: "**Think before you post.**"

## Cisco Social Media Policy

www.slideshare.net/Cisco/cisco-global-social-media-policy?
ref=http://blogs.cisco.com/news/cisco_social_media_guidelines
_policies_and_faq/

Cisco provides another example of best practices. At the heart of the policy is an introduction statement that explains who is affected: "All Cisco employees, vendors and contractors who are creating or contributing to blogs, wikis, social networks, discussion forums, or any other kind of social media—whether on Cisco.com or otherwise."

The policy addresses rules for proper behavior, what people should do if they have questions, why transparency is so important, how to disclose your relationship with the company, and what information should be kept confidential.

## The Oracle Social Media Participation Policy

https://blogs.oracle.com/otn/entry/the_oracle_social_media_partic

The Oracle policy also addresses the wide range of platforms affected and an important reminder that all posts ". . .can have an influence on your ability to conduct your job responsibilities, your teammates' abilities to do their jobs, and Oracle's business interests."

The policy has very clear "requirements" so that there are no misunderstandings, and offers a very clear disclosure statement for Oracle employees with personal blogs: "*The views expressed on this [blog; website] are my own and do not necessarily reflect the views of Oracle.*"

## Intel Social Media Guidelines

www.intel.com/content/www/us/en/legal/intel-social-media-guidelines.html

Intel's policy gets right at the heart of the importance of social media at the start by talking about the importance of social media and the value of interactive business relationships.

The policy provides official guidelines for participating in social media for Intel and makes it clear that as new social networking tools emerge, ". . .the policy will evolve."

Intel's policy addresses honesty, transparency, confidentiality, brand and trademark use, and how to treat the competition with respect. Most important in the policy is this piece of advice: "Add Value."

## NPR Ethics Policy

From: http://ethics.npr.org/tag/social-media/

It is worth sharing the NPR (National Public Radio) Ethics Policy as a best practice because, once again, there are some important takeaways. While this policy is primarily targeted to journalists, there is much we can learn from it.

Some important aspects of the policy address fairness, honesty, and respect, as well as verifying the accuracy of information, and always being careful, especially during breaking news.

The policy also reminds us about images, that images can be manipulated, so before we share images, we should be absolutely certain we are sharing accurate images.

## Resources

### Social Media Disclosure Toolkit | SocialMedia.org

This features a Microsoft Word version with many templates you can download and change to fit your organization.
http://socialmedia.org/disclosure/

### Social Media Policy Database

A database of over 100 social media policies.
http://socialmediagovernance.com/policies/

### The NLRB and Social Media

www.nlrb.gov/news-outreach/fact-sheets/nlrb-and-social-media

### NLRB Website—Protected Concerted Activity

www.nlrb.gov/rights-we-protect/protected-concerted-activity

## American Medical Association Statement on Social Media Ethics

www.ama-assn.org/ama/pub/physician-resources/medical-ethics/code-medical-ethics/opinion9124.page?

## Society of Human Resources Management

## Using Social Media to Boost Ethics and Compliance

www.shrm.org/hrdisciplines/ethics/articles/pages/social-media-ethics-compliance.aspx

## PRSA: Ethical Practice of Social Media in Public Relations

www.instituteforpr.org/research-ethical-practice-social-media-public-relations/

## State Bar of California—Articles: The Law and Social Media

http://ethics.calbar.ca.gov/Ethics/EthicsTechnologyResources/SocialMedia.aspx

## Technology Ethics Articles | The Markkula Center for Applied Ethics

www.scu.edu/ethics/practicing/focusareas/technology/articles.html

# References

## Introduction

Knezevich, C. 2014. "4 Ways Compliance Can Leverage Social Media (Provided Social Media Training Is Included)." Retrieved from: www.jdsupra.com/legalnews/4-ways-compliance-can-leverage-social-me-28654/

Ayres, C. 2009. "Revenge is best served cold – on YouTube: How a broken guitar became a smash hit." *The Sunday Times*.

United Breaks Guitars Video, YouTube, www.youtube.com/watch?v=5YGc4zOqozo

Carroll, D. 2012. *United Breaks Guitars*. Carlsbad, CA: Hay House.

## Chapter 1

PewResearchCenter. 2014. "Social Networking Fact Sheet." Retrieved from: www.pewinternet.org/fact-sheets/social-networking-fact-sheet/

U.S. Department of Commerce and NTIA. 2014. Exploring the Digital Nation. Retrieved from: www.ntia.doc.gov/files/ntia/publications/exploring_the_digital_nation_embracing_the_mobile_internet_10162014.pdf

Shah, Y. 2014. "114-Year-Old Woman Has to Lie About Age to Join Facebook." Retrieved from: www.huffingtonpost.com/2014/10/13/114-year-old-facebook-_n_5977562.html

Guimarães, T. 2014. "The Demographic Trends for Every Social Network." Retrieved from: www.businessinsider.com/2014-social-media-demographics-update-2014-9#ixzz3GdTyRYKI

U.S. Department of Commerce and NTIA. 2014. "Digital Nation Report Shows Rapid Adoption of Mobile Internet Use." Retrieved from: www.commerce.gov/blog/2014/10/16/digital-nation-report-shows-rapid-adoption-mobile-internet-use

Perez, S. 2014. "Majority of Digital Media Consumption Now Takes Place in Mobile Apps." Retrieved from: http://techcrunch.com/2014/08/21/majority-of-digital-media-consumption-now-takes-place-in-mobile-apps/

nielsen.com. 2014a. "The U.S. Digital Consumer Report." Retrieved from: www.nielsen.com/content/corporate/us/en/insights/reports/2014/the-us-digital-consumer-report.html

nielsen.com 2014b. "The Car Is the Information Superhighway." Retrieved from: www.nielsen.com/us/en/insights/news/2014/the-car-is-the-information-superhighway.html

Groenfeldt, T. 2014. "Cash is King No More As Mobile Payments Soar." Retrieved from: www.forbes.com/sites/tomgroenfeldt/2014/10/18/cash-is-king-no-more-as-mobile-payments-soar/

newsroom.mastercard.com. 2014. "13 Million Social Media Conversations Show What Consumers Think about Mobile Payments." Retrieved from: http://newsroom.mastercard.com/press-releases/13-million-social-media-conversations-show-what-consumers-think-about-mobile-payments/

Statistica (2016) Total revenue of global mobile payment market from 2015 to 2019 (in billion U.S. dollars). Retrieved from: http://www.statista.com/statistics/226530/mobile-payment-transaction-volume-forecast/

transactionworld.net. 2014. "Evaluating How Payment Technologies are Converging with Social Media." Retrieved from: www.transactionworld.net/articles/2014/february/mobile.html

Sterling, G. 2014. "Social Media, Mobile and YouTube Changing the Nature of 'TV.'" Retrieved from: http://marketingland.com/social-media-mobile-youtube-changing-nature-tv-79755

researchexcellence.com. 2014. Consumers' Desire To Stream Video Content On TV Screens Will Drive Content Device Purchases, Council For Research Excellence Studies Suggest. Retrieved from: www.researchexcellence.com/documents/news/70.pdf

## Chapter 2

Marsden, P. 2000. "Social Networks." In *Encyclopedia of Sociology*, 2nd ed., edited by E.F. Borgatta, and R.J.V. Montgomery. New York, NY: Macmillan, pp. 2727–35.

Wasserman, S., and K.B. Faust. 1994. *Social Network Analysis: Methods and Applications*. New York, NY: Cambridge University Press.

Pescosolido, B.A., and E.R. Wright. 2004. "The View from Two Worlds: The Convergence of Social Network Reports between Mental Health Clients and Their Ties." *Social Science & Medicine* 58, no. 9, pp. 1795–806.

Knoke, D. 1990. *Political Networks*. New York, NY: Cambridge University Press.

Scott, J., and P.J. Carrington. 2011. *The SAGE Handbook of Social Network Analysis*. Thousand Oaks, CA: SAGE Publications.

Solis, B. 2012. "Social Media Is About Social Science Not Technology." Retrieved from: www.briansolis.com/2012/03/social-media-is-about-social-science-not-technology/

Gallivan, R. 2014. "Amid Fake Reviews, Consumers Are Skeptical of Social Media Marketing." Retrieved from: http://blogs.wsj.com/digits/2014/06/03/amid-fake-reviews-consumers-are-skeptical-of-social-media-marketing/tab/print/?mg=blogs-wsj&url=http%253A%252F%252Fbl%E2%80%A6

Whitler, K.A. 2014. "Why Word of Mouth Marketing Is the Most Important Social Media." Retrieved from: www.forbes.com/sites/kimberlywhitler/2014/07/17/why-word-of-mouth-marketing-is-the-most-important-social-media/

## Chapter 3

ethics.npr.org. n.d. "NPR Social Media Ethics Handbook." Retrieved from: http://ethics.npr.org/tag/social-media/
ethics.org. 2009. "Ethics Glossary." Retrieved from: www.ethics.org/resource/ethics-glossary
ethics.org. 2013 "National Business Ethics Survey®." Retrieved from: www.ethics.org/nbes/
Gentile, M. 2010. "Giving Voice to Values." Retrieved from: www.givingvoicetovaluesthebook.com/about/

## Chapter 4

Brown, T. 2014. "Are Your Tweets Trusted Or Tainted? The Realities of Social Media #Fails." Retrieved from: www.theguardian.com/media/2014/sep/08/tweets-trusted-tainted-social-media-fails
Zaki, C. 2013. "Paying for Followers May Cost You a Job." Retrieved from: www.forbes.com/sites/chereenzaki/2013/03/26/paying-for-followers-may-cost-you-a-job/
Fink, J. 2010. "Five Nurses Fired for Facebook Postings." Retrieved from: http://scrubsmag.com/five-nurses-fired-for-facebook-postings/
Sison, D. 2014. "Singapore Airlines Apologizes to Netizens for Its "Insensitive" and "Unethical" Posts on MH 17 Disaster." Retrieved from: www.chinatopix.com/articles/4452/20140720/singapore-airlines-apologizes-netizens-insensitive-unethical-posts-mh17.htm
Broderick, R. 2013. "Kenneth Cole Decided to Tweet Something Completely Stupid About Syria." Retrieved from: www.buzzfeed.com/ryanhatesthis/kenneth-cole-decided-to-tweet-something-completely
Ray, A. 2013. "Ethics in Social Media Marketing: Responding to the Boston Tragedy." Retrieved from: http://socialmediatoday.com/
mediaethicsafternoon.wordpress.com. 2014. "Unethical Social Media Marketing." Retrieved from: http://mediaethicsafternoon.wordpress.com/2014/02/24/unethical-social-media-marketing/
Fitzpatrick, A. 2012. "NRA Tweet." Retrieved from: http://mashable.com/2012/07/20/nra-tweet/
Wasserman, T. 2012. "Gap Criticized for Insensitive Tweet During Hurricane Sandy." Retrieved from: http://mashable.com/2012/10/31/gap-tweet-hurricane-sandy/

Pinkham, C.A. 2014. "Oh Look, a Company Is Paying People to Post Fake Yelp Reviews." Retrieved from: http://kitchenette.jezebel.com/oh-look-a-company-is-paying-people-to-post-fake-yelp-r-1641909713

Streitfeld, D. 2013. "Give Yourself 5 Stars? Online, It Might Cost You." Retrieved from: www.nytimes.com/2013/09/23/technology/give-yourself-4-stars-online-it-might-cost-you.html?_r=0

nielsen.com. 2012. "Global Trust in Advertising and Brand Messages." Retrieved from: www.nielsen.com/us/en/insights/reports/2012/global-trust-in-advertising-and-brand-messages.html

syncapse.com. 2013. "The Value of a Facebook Fan 2013." Retrieved from: www.syncapse.com/value-of-a-facebook-fan-2013/#.VB8O1StdWl8

BrightLocal.com. 2014. "Local Consumer Review Survey 2014." Retrievedfrom: www.brightlocal.com/2014/07/01/local-consumer-review-survey-2014/

Pan, J. 2012. "By 2014, 1 in 10 Social Media Reviews Will Be Fake [STUDY]." Retrieved from: http://mashable.com/2012/09/20/fake-online-reviews/

Harvardmagazine.com. 2011. "HBS Study Finds Positive Yelp Reviews Boost Business." Retrieved from: http://harvardmagazine.com/2011/10/hbs-study-finds-positive-yelp-reviews-lead-to-increased-business

gartner.com. 2012. "Gartner Says By 2014, 10-15 Percent of Social Media Reviews to Be Fake, Paid for By Companies." Retrieved from: www.gartner.com/newsroom/id/2161315

Fuscaldo, D. 2014. "How to Spot Fake Online Reviews." Retrieved from: www.foxbusiness.com/personal-finance/2014/06/27/how-to-spot-fake-online-reviews/

Tadena, M. 2014. "Advertising-Wary Consumers Still Turn to Word-of-Mouth Marketing." Retrieved from: http://blogs.wsj.com/cmo/2014/10/14/advertising-wary-consumers-still-turn-to-word-of-mouth-marketing/

Fisman, R. 2012. "Should You Trust Online Reviews?" Retrieved from: www.slate.com/articles/business/the_dismal_science/2012/08/tripadvisor_expedia_yelp_amazon_are_online_reviews_trustworthy_economists_weigh_in_.single.html

Desta, Y. 2014. "How to Spot a Fake Review." Retrieved from: http://mashable.com/2014/05/29/fake-online-reviews-tips/

Miller, J.A. 2015. "Are Fake Online Reviews Crushing Consumer Confidence?" Retrieved from: www.cio.com/article/3009686/marketing/are-fake-online-reviews-crushing-consumer-confidence.html

Wattles, J. 2015. "Amazon Sues More Than 1,000 Sellers of "Fake" Product Reviews." Retrieved from: http://money.cnn.com/2015/10/18/technology/amazon-lawsuit-fake-reviews/

# Chapter 5

Lauby, S. 2012. "Ethics and Social Media: Where Should You Draw the Line?" Retrieved from: www.americanexpress.com/us/small-business/openforum/articles/ethics-and-social-media-where-should-you-draw-the-line/

TLNT.com. 2014. "More Employers Not Hiring Due to What They Find on Social Media." Retrieved from: www.tlnt.com/2014/06/26/more-employers-not-hiring-due-to-what-they-find-on-social-media/

Spraggins, C. 2014. "The Pros and Cons of Using Social Media for Candidate Screening." Retrieved from: www.payscale.com/compensation-today/2014/08/the-pros-and-cons-of-using-social-media-for-candidate-screening

insurancequotes.org. 2014. "Your Social Media Could Affect Your Insurance Rates." Retrieved from: www.insurancequotes.org/auto/your-social-media-could-affect-your-insurance-rates/

American Medical News. 2010. "Social Media Pose Ethical Unknowns for Doctors." Retrieved from: www.amednews.com/article/20100906/profession/309069944/2/

Goldmann, P. 2012. "Social Media Sites: The Fraud Investigator's New Best Friend . . . But "Friending" Can Be Risky." Retrieved from: www.acfe.com/fraud-examiner.aspx?id=4294971928

Sherman, E. 2013. "6 Most Outrageous Social Media Mistakes by Teachers." Retrieved from: http://jobs.aol.com/articles/2013/06/18/teachers-social-media-mistakes/

Broderick, R. 2013. "10 People Who Learned Social Media Can Get You Fired." Retrieved from: www.cnn.com/2013/06/06/living/buzzfeed-social-media-fired/

Huhman, H.R. 2013. "6 Reasons Social Media Got People Fired." Retrieved from: www.businessinsider.com/6-reasons-social-media-got-people-fired-2013-7

ethicsinpr.wikispaces.com. n.d. "Ghost Blogging." Retrieved from: http://ethicsinpr.wikispaces.com/Ghost+blogging

BWGlaw.net. 2014. "Use of Social Media in the Courtroom." Retrieved from: http://bwglaw.net/social-media-in-the-courtroom/

Crank, J. 2013. "Most Social Media Users Unaware Posts Can Be Used in Court." Retrieved from: http://blogs.lawyers.com/2013/07/social-media-used-against-you/

Callahan, D.G. 2012. "Social Media Posts Admissible in Court." Retrieved from: www.journal-news.com/news/news/social-media-posts-admissible-in-court/nSWR3/

maleyinvestigations.com. 2014. "Child Custody: Family Court and Social Media." Retrieved from: http://maleyinvestigations.com/child-custody.asp?tip=45

Hall, P. 2014. "Jurors' Social Media Posts a Growing Threat to Fair Trials." Retrieved from www.policeone.com/court/articles/7317344-Jurors-social-media-posts-a-growing-threat-to-fair-trials/

drewcochranlaw.com. 2014. "Can My Facebook Post Be Used Against Me in Court?" Retrieved from: http://drewcochranlaw.com/can-facebook-post-used-court/

# Chapter 6

Federal Trade Commission. 2013. "comDisclosures: How to Make Effective Disclosures in Digital Advertising." Retrieved from: www.ftc.gov/sites/default/files/attachments/press-releases/ftc-staff-revises-online-advertising-disclosure-guidelines/130312dotcomdisclosures.pdf

Myers, C. 2014. "#Disclosure: New FTC Social Media Guidelines for PR." Retrieved from: www.instituteforpr.org/disclosure-new-ftc-social-media-guidelines-pr-practice/

# Chapter 7

Pearce, Pat sipandnosh.com. 2014. "NLRB Ruling Shows Need for Caution When Addressing Employee Social Media Use." Retrieved from: http://sipandnosh.com/nlrb-ruling-shows-need-for-caution-when-addressing-employee-social-media-use/

# Chapter 8

Pollitt, C. 2013. "How Companies Can Implement and Benefit from a Social Media Governance Policy." Retrieved from: www.huffingtonpost.com/chad-pollitt/how-companies-can-impleme_b_4297187.html

Demetrio. 2013. "5 Practical Tips: Implementing a Social Media Policy at your organization." Retrieved from: www.limeredstudio.com/what-we-think/5-practical-tips-implementing-a-social-media-policy-at-your-organization/#.VAI4r0tvkQc

Meister, J. 2012. "Social Media Training Is Now Mandatory: Five Ways to Make Sure Your Company Does It Right." Retrieved from: www.forbes.com/sites/jeannemeister/2012/10/31/social-media-training-is-now-mandatory/

Tung, E.T. 2014. "How to Write a Social Media Policy to Empower Employees." Retrieved from: www.socialmediaexaminer.com/write-a-social-media-policy/

DiResta. 2013. "Understanding the FTC's Disclosure Guidelines." Retrieved from: www.womma.org/posts/2013/08/understanding-the-ftcs-disclosure-guidelines

# Chapter 9

Mataconis, D. 2014. "Suing Customers Who Give Bad Reviews." www .outsidethebeltway.com/suing-customers-who-give-bad-reviews/ Chapter 10

Peterson, H. 2013. "A Southwest Airlines Worker Sued a Passenger Over Tweets Blasting Customer Service." Retrieved from: www.businessinsider. com/nashville-singer-is-sued-for-angry-tweets-about-southwest-airlines-2013-10#ixzz3HygjxRnL

Crabtree, T., Krasnow, M., Lewis, J., Nafziger, J., van Hoosear, J., and L. Zadra-Symes. 2014. "Legal Perspective on Negative Online Reviews: What Both Sides Should Consider Before Jumping Into the Fray." Retrieved from: www .jdsupra.com/legalnews/legal-perspective-on-negative-online-rev-07923/

# Chapter 10

Valentino-Devries, J., and J. Singer-Vine. 2012. "They Know What You're Shopping For." Retrieved from: http://online.wsj.com/articles/SB100014241278 873247844045781431441132736214

Angwin, J., and J. Valentino-Devries.2012. "New Tracking Frontier: Your License Plates." Retrieved from: http://online.wsj.com/news/articles/SB10000872396390443995604578004723603576296?mg=reno64-wsj&url=http%3A%2F%2Fonline.wsj.com%2Farticle%2FSB10000872396390443995604578004723603576296.html

Greenberg, E., and A. Kates. 2013. *Strategic Digital Marketing: Top Digital Experts Share the Formula for Tangible Returns on Your Marketing Investment.* Kindle ed. New York, NY: McGraw-Hill, pp. 253–254.

Martin, C. 2013. *Mobile Influence: The New Power of the Consumer (Kindle Locations 2997-3000).* Kindle ed. New York, NY: Palgrave Macmillan.

Levitt, J. 2014. "In-Store Cell Phone Tracking Pits Consumers Against Retailers." Retrieved from: http://adage.com/article/digitalnext/store-cell-phone-tracking-pits-consumers-stores/292628/

Myers,C.2014."#Disclosure:NewFTCSocialMediaGuidelinesforPR."Retrievedfrom: www.instituteforpr.org/disclosure-new-ftc-social-media-guidelines-pr-practice/

SocialMedia.org. 2014. "Archive of the SocialMedia.org Disclosure Toolkit." Retrieved from: http://socialmedia.org/disclosure/

# Index

# THE GIVING VOICE TO VALUES ON BUSINESS ETHICS AND CORPORATE SOCIAL RESPONSIBILITY COLLECTION

Mary Gentile, *Editor*

The Giving Voice To Values initiative teamed up with Business Expert Press to produce a collection of books on Business Ethics and Corporate Social Responsibility that will bring a practical, solutions-oriented, skill-building approach to the salient questions of values-driven leadership. Giving Voice To Values (www.GivingVoiceToValues.org)—the curriculum, the pedagogy and the research upon which it is based—was designed to transform the foundational assumptions upon which the teaching of business ethics is based, and importantly, to equip future business leaders to not only know what is right, but how to make it happen.

## Other Titles in This Collection

- *Ethical Leadership in Sport: What's Your ENDgame?* by Pippa Grange
- *The ART of Responsible Communication: Leading With Values Every Day* by David L. Remund
- *Engaging Millennials for Ethical Leadership: What Works For Young Professionals and Their Managers* by Jessica McManus Warnell
- *Sales Ethics: How To Sell Effectively While Doing the Right Thing* by Alberto Aleo and Alice Alessandri
- *Working Ethically in Finance: Clarifying Our Vocation* by Anthony Asher
- *A Strategic and Tactical Approach to Global Business Ethics, Second Edition* by Lawrence A. Beer
- *Shaping the Future of Work: What Future Worker, Business, Government, and Education Leaders Need To Do For All To Prosper* by Thomas A. Kochan
- *War Stories: Fighting, Competing, Imagining, Leading* by Leigh Hafrey

## Announcing the Business Expert Press Digital Library

*Concise e-books business students need for classroom and research*

This book can also be purchased in an e-book collection by your library as

- *a one-time purchase,*
- *that is owned forever,*
- *allows for simultaneous readers,*
- *has no restrictions on printing, and*
- *can be downloaded as PDFs from within the library community.*

Our digital library collections are a great solution to beat the rising cost of textbooks. E-books can be loaded into their course management systems or onto students' e-book readers.
The **Business Expert Press** digital libraries are very affordable, with no obligation to buy in future years. For more information, please visit **www.businessexpertpress.com/librarians.**
To set up a trial in the United States, please email **sales@businessexpertpress.com**

CPSIA information can be obtained
at www.ICGtesting.com
Printed in the USA
LVHW020015040322
712557LV00011B/1532

9 781606 498521